MAMATOTO

MAMATOTO

MAMATOTO

MAMATOTO

AMATOTO

MAMATOTO

D0565900

We two form a multitude - Ovid

MAMATOTO

A CELEBRATION OF BIRTH

The Body Shop Team

Carroll Dunham
Frances Myers
Neil Barnden
Alan McDougall
Thomas L. Kelly
with
Barbara Aria

virago

Published by VIRAGO PRESS Limited 1991
20-23 Mandela St, Camden Town, London
NW1 0HQ

Copyright © 1991 THE BODY SHOP
International PLC, Hawthorn Road, Wick,
Littlehampton, West Sussex BN17 7LR

The right of The Body Shop to be identified
as the author of this work has been asserted
in accordance with the Copyright, Designs and
Patents Act 1988 and have not waived their
right to object to derogatory treatment of the work.

All rights reserved

*A CIP catalogue record for this book is
available from the British Library*

Printed and bound in Germany by
Mohndruck GmbH, Gütersloh
Colour separation by C.L.G.,
Via C. Betteloni 19, Verona, Italy

CONTENTS

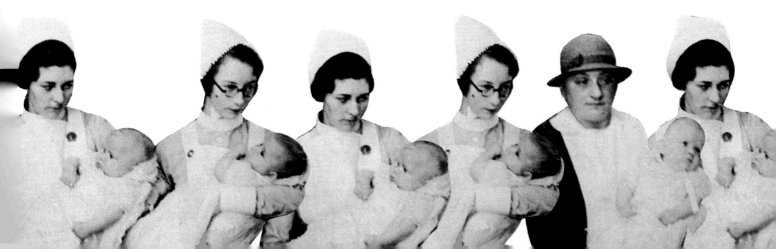

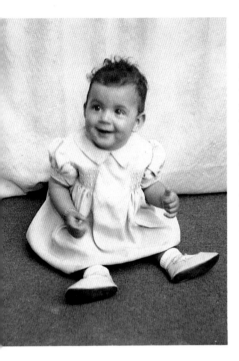

INTRODUCTION

Frequent travels south of the equator, where I gossiped and shared life stories with women, made me realize that there was a wealth of knowledge about birth, virtually hidden from us in the Western world. I was amazed by the lore - their stories about conception, pregnancy, birth and babycare are so different from our own cultural experience. It made me wonder: what do we share with women in other lands? And what can our ancestors teach us?

We began gathering stories from indigenous cultures and scouring our own past for gleanings. Let me tell you, my entire soul was riveted by these stories. I never knew about the practices other cultures have devised to care for their emotions - practices they have carried out for centuries, uninterrupted by science and technology. Many of these rituals and stories informed the creation of our mother-and-baby range of products called Mamatoto, which in Swahili means motherbaby.

So much of the information we gathered made so much sense to me that I can't help but ask why it is not considered 'real knowledge'. At best,

it is absolutely accurate, at worst, curiously interesting.Upon reflection, I find little interesting in the science of birth. To me, the information is like advertising - prescriptive and one way. What pleases me about this book and about the lore it collects is that the information here is more like a conversation or a dialogue which sparks debate.

All I remember now of my last birth experience over twenty years ago is a nurse yelling at the doctor about being bloody insensitive as he sewed me up while I lay prone on the table. What choices did I have? Why did I have to give up control of my body? We didn't know what alternatives there were, what birth was like in other lands. The more I have learned since, the more outraged I have become. I am outraged that far too many women have given up their bodies to hospitals without a fight. I am outraged that obsolete Western obstetric technology is dumped in Third World countries. I am outraged that in litigious America malpractice and the medical establishment threaten to banish midwifery to the history books. I am outraged that we assume the 'scientific' method is superior to the practical knowledge women have gained over a millennia of birth experience.

But my sense of irretrievable loss is only part of the tragedy that haunts birth. Birth is not always a comfortable experience, and the black pages at the end of each chapter are a silent howl of injustice at the shockingly real tragedies that exist side by side with our personal sense of joy. Though essentially celebratory in nature, this is not always a comfortable book.

These Mamatoto stories so satiated my curiosity buds that I'm jealous I didn't know them sooner. If only my husband Gordon had whispered sweet nothings in my ear like a Dogon lover and made me calm and content as a Nyinba mother, perhaps my daughters would not have been born so argumentative! I find *Mamatoto* immensely entertaining, and its commonsense wisdom shocking. I have learned so much from this diverse pageantry of what it means to give birth that my mind swims with possibilities. I have faith that my daughters will know their own bodies

better, that they will make more creative and educated choices about giving birth than I ever could. Walt Whitman's words forever resonate: 're-examine all you have been told ... dismiss what insults your soul.'

I hope *Mamatoto* will help us re-examine all we have been told and remind us of what we might already know: that by caring for our bodies and our babies' bodies through the most elemental language of touch - through massage, aromatherapy, bathing and breastfeeding - we can begin to fulfil our hopes for a gentler future.

ANITA RODDICK, FOUNDER AND GROUP MANAGING DIRECTOR OF THE BODY SHOP

Anita Roddick

Editor's Note:
Sometimes ideas change faster than language. For lack of better alternatives we have reluctantly used the terms *Western*, *indigenous*, *Third World*, *industrial* and *non-industrial* to convey complex notions of diverse cultures. May our children find words that are far more precise.

WHERE HAVE YOU COME FROM, LITTLE ONE?
WHERE WERE YOU STAYING BEFORE?
TODAY, WHERE HAVE YOU MADE YOUR CAMP.

I CAME FROM THE SKY;
TILL NOW I WAS STAYING IN THE BELLY
TODAY I HAVE CAMPED ON EARTH.
(Sung by the Chholar Mangal of India
on the birth of a child)

I

CAME

FROM

THE

SKY

The mystery of conception has puzzled humans since the dawn of time. Ever since our hairy ancestors on the savannah plains first scratched their heads with emergent philosophical musings, people throughout history and all over the world have come up with answers that poetically express the sense of miracle we still feel when we realize we have made a baby.

In rarefied moments of silence, when dawn light filters gently through the canopy of an Amazon forest, or grey

mist hangs thick and heavy on a Scottish coast, or an African night sky explodes with a flurry of shooting stars over a parched desert, simple questions can resonate in the wind: Where do we come from? Are we sent by God, as many people believe, or does the stork deliver us? Do we come from the sky or from the earth?

Women and men all over the world, and throughout history, have created ways of understanding the genesis of life which springs forth from our bodies. With the stirrings of the new life within her, a pregnant woman particularly wonders at the mystery and miracle of creation.

We in the Western world don't believe that babies come from the earth, as Australian Aborigines do, nor from the sky. And yet, with all our advanced knowledge about eggs and sperm and DNA, the intricate process of conception and

The babies were little stars from Spiritland, and ... when they first came to the earth ... they were from the sky and nameless. (Osage Indians)

Evening Star, you bring all things which the bright dawn has scattered. You bring the sheep, you bring the goat, you bring the child back to its mother. (Sappho, 612 B.C).

10

germination takes place inside our bodies without us being remotely aware of it. You could have been drinking a cup of coffee or stuck in a traffic jam just at that point, anywhere from about three to thirty-six hours after making love, when the sperm cell entered the ovum. In fact, our experience of conception is not so very different to the experience of women and men all over the world. We can't see it, we can't feel it, and although we know the theory, we don't know all the answers. We can only assume. Just as the Kanuri man in North Borneo assumed when he said that his wife got pregnant because they experienced simultaneous orgasm: 'How else can a woman conceive a baby?'

Why did you get pregnant this time, and not another time? The baby that will be born out of your body after nine months was the result of a chance meeting of one particular sperm and one particular egg - a meeting less likely than the chance meeting of two people born at opposite ends of the world. Why, out of up to two hundred million sperm cells, did this specific one, with its specific genetic stucture, fuse with this specific egg to create this individual baby?

What might you have been doing at that point in time when your child's genetic destiny was being written? (In India, it's traditional to keep vigil on the sixth night after birth, when the Goddess is believed to visit the child and write its destiny on its forehead.)

WHO LIVES IN YOU
AND QUICKENS TO LIFE LIKE LAST
YEAR'S MELON SEEDS?
ARE YOU YOUR FATHER'S FATHER,
OR HIS BROTHER,
OR YET ANOTHER?
WHOSE SPIRIT IS THAT THAT IS IN
YOU, LITTLE WARRIOR?
(Didinga naming song, East Africa)

Have you wondered who this child-in-the-making will take after - whose genes are forming its eyes, its feet, the shape of its nose, the facets of its personality? From conception, a child is genetically destined to carry into the future the traits of its forebears - a phenomenon that's reflected in the idea of reincarnation.

An Australian Aborigine bark painting depicts the ancient Earth Mother giving birth to spirit babies.

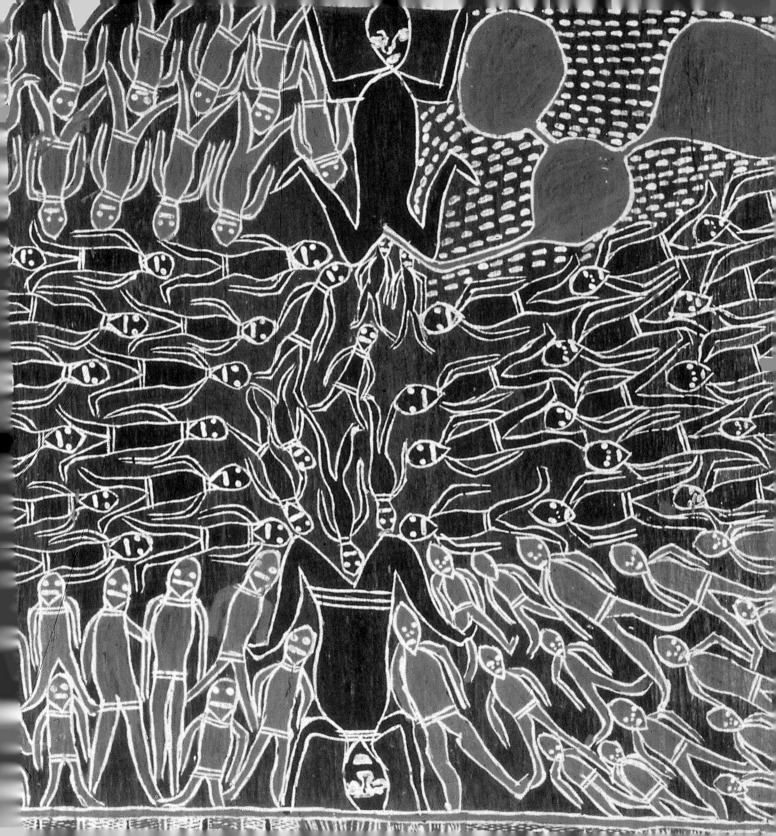

Where did you
come from,
baby dear?
Out of the
everywhere into
the here.
Where did you
get your eyes so
blue?
Out of the sky
as I came
through.
(George
MacDonald)

THE POWER OF WORDS

The Dogon people of Western Africa hold what must be one of the most poetic of all conception theories: they believe in the power of words to make babies. Every time a Dogon man utters a word heard by a woman, he is contributing to her fertility. To impregnate a woman, a man must gently whisper the ancient stories of the ancestors into her ear before making love. His words will enter her ear, pass through her throat and liver, and spiral around her womb, where they form the celestial germ of water that can receive a man's seed.

In many cultures, birth and death are mysteries that follow upon one another in an eternal cycle, so that the story of life has no beginning or ending and the child who makes the belly swell is not new life, but life renewed. On the birth of an Ainu child in Japan, the grandfather is remembered with the expression, 'He did not die, he fell into the womb of his daughter.'

People in some parts of Africa and Asia believe that spirit children live in special, ancestral homes. Western science tells us that a girl's body is provided at birth with four hundred thousand eggs - a lifetime of potential children. The Aborigines believe that the ancient Earth Mother long ago created all the spirit babies that were ever to be born in the world, and placed them not in the ovaries but at sacred sites near streams, mountains, caves and gum trees. Here, the spirit children wait to enter a woman who passes by, so that they can be born out of her and become a part of earthly life. (Of course, women who don't want to get pregnant avoid these places whenever possible - and if they can't, they disguise themselves as old women!)

The Tapirape Indians of Brazil believe that the spirit babies choose their temporary womb homes very carefully - almost as if each mother and her baby were meant for each other. The spirit baby curls up in different women's wombs to see which one fits it perfectly. According to a Tapirape shaman, whose job it is ceremoniously to guide the spirits to different potential mothers, the spirit babies are known to say, 'No, I don't think I'll stay here,' or 'This is just right, I'll take this woman to be my mother.'

12

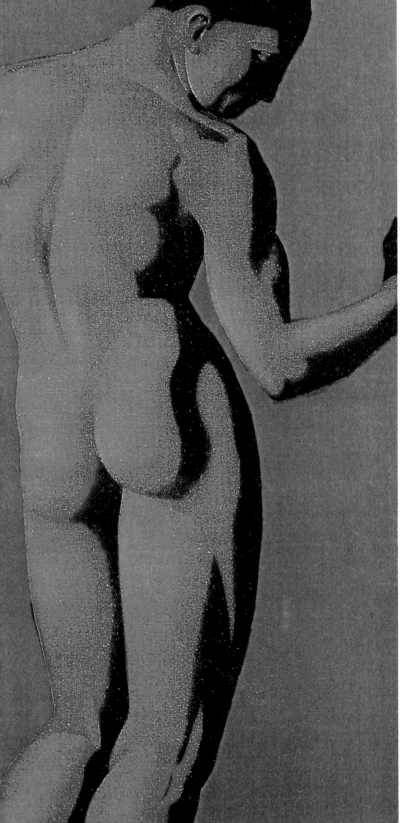

BY MAN ALONE?

Our theories about conception often reflect our attitudes towards the roles of men and women in society. It would be hard to find a modern Western woman who was prepared to accept the theory that she had played no part in the making of the baby in her womb, yet for thousands of years that's exactly what Europeans believed.

When Hippocrates, the great physician of Ancient Greece, suggested that menstrual blood accumulating in the womb during pregnancy might form the baby's flesh - explaining why babies look like both parents - Aristotle whole-heartedly disagreed: only male semen could be responsible for making life. During the second century AD another Greek physician, Galen, proposed a brand - new theory challenging Aristotle: he believed that women contained 'prefab' embryos in their uterus. When semen was ejaculated inside them, it broke the casing surrounding this prefab embryo, enabling it to grow into a baby. But since nobody really knew what the uterus was and nobody had seen a woman's reproductive organ, the

13

theory was rejected. Not until the late 1800s was woman's role in conception acknowledged in the West.

People in some cultures today still believe that only men can be responsible for conception. The woman is just a 'borrowed womb' harbouring the growing life until it's ready to join the man's world. Among the Malay people, for instance, who see man as the higher, rational being, the baby is believed to begin life in the father's brain. There the fetus develops for forty days before sinking down into the father's penis, to be ejected into the mother's dark and earthy womb during intercourse.

On the other hand, some people deny the father any role in the conception of children. Among the Ashanti, a matriarchal society of West Africa, babies are believed to be made entirely from their mothers' menstrual blood. The Imerina and Betsileo people of Madagascar believe that a girl's first intercourse sets off her cycle of childbearing, but that after this first time she no longer needs a man to help her bear children.

In Western science today, popular ideas about conception are influenced by our ideas about man-woman relationships. We tend to think of the fusion of sperm and egg as some sort of romantic meeting of opposites, or even as the vigorous sperm fighting its way up to the waiting egg and forcing itself in. In fact, conception is now believed to be less a matter of male conquest and more like a 'big hairy egg grabs tiny sperm' scenario. The egg - the largest cell in a woman's body - is, in fact, about thirty times larger than a sperm cell, which is the smallest cell in a man's body.

Swimming around blindly in the Fallopian tube, several sperm bump haphazardly into the egg and immediately start wriggling as if trying to escape being trapped in its jelly-like outer layer. Only after the egg has sent out a 'seductive' chemical signal do the sperm stop struggling and start secreting a fluid that eats a hole through the jelly into the centre of the egg. As soon as the sperm closest to the hole has entered the egg, the jelly solidifies, trapping this sperm inside and the others outside. And so the story begins.

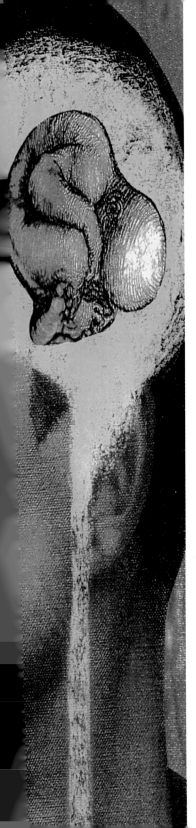

WHAT'S LOVE GOT TO DO WITH IT?

What follows about twelve hours later is far more romantic, as the minute strands of the egg's and sperm's DNA reach across to each other, touch, and match up to create the unique life form that will be the child.

It's because we reproduce sexually, rather than cloning ourselves asexually like amoebas, that we are each so different from one another - and why your baby could have more in common genetically with the baby now nestling in the belly of a tribeswoman thousands of miles away in New Guinea than with the baby next door.

But although most people in the world believe that having sexual intercourse is what makes babies, there are many different theories to explain why.

While conducting interviews for this book, a childless researcher asked Sita, a Nepalese tribeswoman working in the fields, 'How do you get pregnant?' Sita, mother of nine children, rolled on the ground with laughter: 'You *bedeshis* [foreigners] have so few children and start when

you are so old ... Don't you know how? When a man and a woman begin to make love, the souls of people who have died in the last forty days hover around them, because the souls like the man's buttermilk [semen]. When the man's penis enters the woman's body, one soul slips in with it to taste the buttermilk. Once the soul has entered the woman, the buttermilk makes the bones of the baby's body and the woman's menstrual blood makes the flesh.'

There are a few groups of people in the world who make no link between sexual intercourse and conception, believing for instance, as some South African tribeswomen do, that if they lie down in a shower of rain their seeds will be germinated. Before World War II, Trobriand Islanders of the South Pacific believed that although sexual intercourse prepared a woman's body for conception, it was while bathing in the ocean that she actually conceived. Babies were believed to come from the sacred seaweed found floating in the water - not such a strange concept given the scientific theories about life first coming from the sea!

SEED ANIMALS

In sixteenth-century Italy, an anatomist named Gabriello Fallopio, searching in vain for semen in the ovaries, discovered, leading to the uterus, a pair of tubes, now named after him. Once again, the father's role in babymaking prevailed, and when a few years later the student of a great lensmaker, Antony Van Leeuwenhoek, discovered 'little animacules' swimming madly in a sample of semen, the proof seemed sure. Semen, it was proclaimed, contains spermatozoa - seed animals. Scientists ran riot with this new information. Gazing through their microscopes, they believed they saw tiny men in samples of male sperm, and tiny donkeys were reported sighted in donkey sperm.

One of the most whimsical experiments was conducted a hundred years later by a famous Italian biologist of the time, who dressed up some male frogs in taffeta trousers so that when they met with female frogs their sperm would get caught up in the trousers instead of in the deposit of female eggs. He then took some of the entrapped semen, mixed it with the female eggs, and

MONSTER SOUP commonly called THAMES WATER, being a correct representation of that precious stuff, doled out to us !!!

hey presto! The eggs became fertilized. Proof, the biologist insisted, that man's sperm was capable of causing the tiny tadpole waiting in each egg to grow.

It wasn't until late in the last century that two German anatomists - one studying a starfish, the other a sea urchin - finally came to the conclusion that women have an equal part in the process of conception when they saw for the first time a sperm penetrating an egg, resulting in the fusion of two cells to form one new cell: a baby in the making. The first meeting of egg and sperm.

CHILDREN COME AS THE RAIN

The record -holder for most children born to one mother is a Russian woman who produced 69 children between 1725 and 1765: 16 pairs of twins, 7 sets of triplets, and 4 sets of quadruplets. The modern record-holder is Leontina Albina of Chile, who by 1980 had produced 44 children.

The fertility of the earth is often associated with the fruitfulness of women's bodies to bear babies. A Newar woman sifts wheat. Bhaktapur, Nepal.

The Mixtecan Indians of Mexico have a saying, 'Children come as the rain.' Where life is lived close to the land, and survival depends on seeds germinating in the rain-soaked earth, fertility takes on a special meaning. In agricultural societies, having children is not only as natural a part of life as the sowing and reaping of crops, but equally crucial too. As the Mixtecan people say: without water, the crops would die; and without children, life in the community could not continue.

The connection between the fruitfulness of the land and the fruitfulness of woman is forever being made in the rites practised by people who live by cultivating. When we throw confetti at the bride and groom as they leave the wedding, we are enacting the vestige of just such a rite - once upon a time it was rice that was thrown, with the idea that the plant's fertility would transfer to whomever it touched. Fertility associations are entrenched in our culture and we continue to uphold the traditions even though the origin and meanings have been lost. For example, the plant baby's breath

(gypsophila), symbolizing fertility, is still traditionally used in a bride's bouquet, and old shoes - thought to be symbolic of female sex organs, believed to signify many children - are still tied to the rear of the bride and bridegroom's car in parts of Europe.

In Indonesia, where the link between fertile land and the mother's seedbed is still alive, the ripening rice crop is treated just like a pregnant woman. No one must make a sudden noise or cause a disturbance that might upset the grain until it is harvested.

For many women, having a baby is the only the thing that can bring not only status in the community, but personal fulfilment too. Even in our own culture, where children aren't needed to prove a family's wealth or to help work the land, where women have many avenues to self-fulfilment and can usually choose when - and whether - to have a baby, many women reach a point in their lives at which the yearning to become a mother, to experience her own fruitfulness, puts everything else in shadow. The recent development of artificial insemination and *in vitro* fertilization, while raising a whole new set of moral and ethical issues, also offers men and women a hope for conception that their ancestors could never have dreamed about.

Amongst mobile, foraging cultures such as the !Kung of Botswana, children are not economic necessities (in fact too many children make life difficult), yet the experience of birth is seen as changing a woman for ever. Among the Lapps of Lappland and some African societies, parents are renamed after their firstborn children - mother of Oba or father of Ayo - because in becoming parents they have become new people, and need new names to reflect their new role.

THE DELIGHTS OF LOVE

The inability to conceive has long been seen as a medical problem in our own culture. Through the centuries, all sorts of complicated 'medical' remedies have been prescribed; in 1783 *The Compleat Housewife* recommended a brew made of ale, ox-backs, catmint, dates and raisins, nutmegs, and the 'syrup of stinking orris', to be taken cheerfully every night out of sight of the husband. Around the same time a certain James Graham, so-called doctor, created a Temple of Health in London where childless couples could enjoy 'the delights of love' in a Grand Celestial Bed. The bed, scented with balm, rose leaves, lavender and oriental spices, was specially designed so that it could be tilted to any angle, the idea being that the man's sperm would more easily reach the uterus, causing 'Immediate conception, accompanied by soft music'.

CONTRACEPTION - FROM HONEY TO THE EARL OF CONDOM

An Ancient Egyptian woman had almost as many contraceptive choices as the woman of today - several which have proved to be effective. She could fumigate her genitals with emmer grains or insert a lint tampon soaked in herbal liquid and honey. This liquid, made from acacia tips, produces a lactic acid, which is used today as a natural spermicide. But the most popular method for Egyptians was to insert into the vagina a mixture of crocodile dung, sour milk, and honey. Was it the acidity of the dung or the honey's viscosity (acting as a natural barrier) which made this method so effective?

By the fourth century BC Aristotle recommended cedar oil, white lead or frankicense smeared on the female genitals, while Pliny suggested rubbing sticky cedar gum over the penis to prevent conception.

The South African Djuka tribe, was quite advanced in its thinking about contraception. Djuka women placed a vegetable-seed pod inside themselves to trap the sperm.

Women of the Kasai Basin in central Africa created a cervical plug made of grass.

In Ancient Persia women soaked natural sea sponges with alcohol, iodine, quinine or carbolic acid and inserted them before intercourse.

Fruits have also played their part in contraception. Greek doctors used to scoop out the seeds of a pomegranate half to create a cervical cap, and the famous lover Casanova was well-known for giving his amours partially squeezed lemons.

Amulets of mule's earwax were especially popular amongst Greeks and Romans. During the Middle Ages a drink of tea made from parsley and lavender was believed to prevent pregnancy, as was a good douse of vinegar on the penis.

The condom - known since Roman times - was widely used in Europe by the seventeenth-century. Fallopio designed the first medicated linen sheath in the 1500s and it was the Earl of Condom, the personal physician to King Charles II, who, by trying to prevent his philandering Royal Highness from contracting syphilis, gave the item its name.

Thai fertility statues at the San Chao Mae Tap Tim shrine.

21

MOON ROMANCE

Why is moonlight so romantic? Many of the goddesses connected with fertility around the world are associated with the moon. Amongst certain Latin American people, for instance, a pomegranate is bought in the name of Yemaya, moon goddess and patroness of motherhood. The fruit is cut in half and covered in honey, and the name of the woman who hopes to conceive is written on a piece of paper and wedged between the two pomegranate halves while the moon goddess's name is invoked. The idea is for the woman to become like the pomegranate: ripe with seeds.

People in many cultures believe that when the menstrual blood stops flowing it means that it is accumulating in the woman's belly, forming the 'meaty' part of the baby's body, while the father's semen forms the bones and brains. In the early days of Western civilization, Pliny, the Greek natural philosopher, was a firm believer in this theory. The !Kung bushmen of the Kalahari Desert say that a woman gets pregnant when a man 'cuts her from her moon' - meaning that she can conceive only by making love at the end of her period, when the last of her menstrual blood mixes with her lover's semen to form the child.

*Left:
Neolithic fertility
stone believed to be
used as a calendar
to count the moons
of pregnancy.*

Temple struts on the Basantapur temple in Kathmandu instruct householders in the delights of lovemaking.

WEEKEND SEX

Infrequent sex, because of health problems, fatigue, different work schedules, or sexual problems, can actually diminish your chances of conceiving. Weekend sex can become the norm if both partners work in high-pressure jobs; this can be counter-productive to efforts to become pregnant.

BOY OR GIRL?

What are the chances of your child being a boy or a girl? Surprisingly, the answer is not fifty:fifty. Girls should have an advantage over boys, because for every ten sperm carrying X 'female' chromosomes there are only nine bearing Y 'male' chromosomes. Yet every year more boys than girls are conceived and born (a ratio of ten boys to nine girls). Scientists now believe that this is because Y-bearing sperm are faster than X-bearing sperm at fertilizing eggs.

Can you influence the sex of your child at conception? The Ancient Greeks believed you could conceive boys if you tied up or cut off your left testicle because they thought male sperm was produced in the right testicle. Henry VIII might have been interested in some ancient and current theories, though if he had known that women can provide only the X-chromosome (boys are dependent on the man's sperm), several of his wives might have had happier and longer lives. Some people believe that you can determine which sex of baby you'll have by eating certain foods, or by making love in a certain way. According to Welsh folklore, lying on your right side during intercourse will produce a girl, while lying on your left will bring a boy. The Newars of Nepal traditionally believe that if you make love on an even day of their calendar you will give birth to a boy, while a girl will be produced if you make love on an odd day.

It might be a matter of going to certain, sacred places. Amongst the Zuni tribe of Native Americans, for instance, a couple who wanted a girl child would go to a shrine named Mother Rock, a piece of mountain inscribed with vulva symbols. There, the woman would scrape a small amount of rock to deposit in a tiny vase, which she would leave in a special hole in the rock while she and the father-to-be prayed for a beautiful daughter, a fine weaver, a skilful potter. Boys could be ensured by visiting another shrine higher up the mountain.

Facts You Don't Want To Know

INFERTILITY IS INCREASING

INFERTILITY RATES IN THE WEST ARE SKYROCKETING. THE WORLD HEALTH ORGANIZATION REPORTS THAT ONE IN TEN COUPLES WORLDWIDE ARE INVOLUNTARILY INFERTILE. IN THE UNITED STATES THE RATE IS HIGHER THAN ONE IN SIX, AND THAT'S MORE THAN TWICE AS HIGH AS IT WAS TEN YEARS AGO.

WHY?

THERE ARE SEVERAL SUSPECTED REASONS FOR THIS INFERTILITY EPIDEMIC, INCLUDING THE RAPID SPREAD OF VENEREAL DISEASE, AND THE WIDESPREAD USE OF THE PILL AND IUD. IN THE 1970S RESEARCHERS BEGAN TO NOTICE THAT MEN IN THE UNITED STATES WERE PRODUCING LESS SPERM. SCIENTISTS ARE POINTING TO MODERN STRESS, AND TO ENVIRONMENTAL POLLUTION.

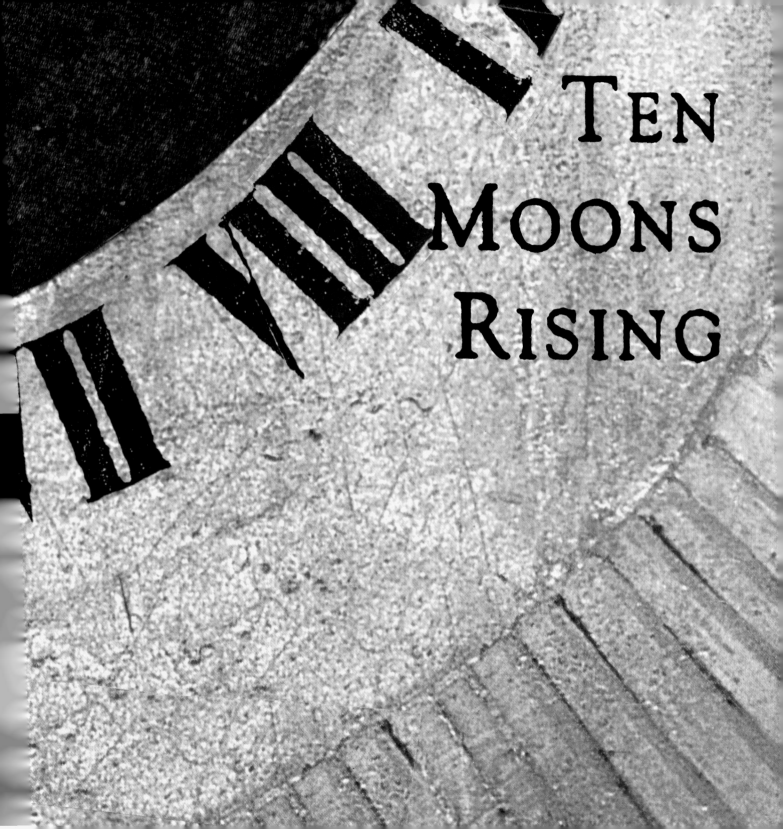

TEN
MOONS
RISING

As a crescent moon rises in the sky over a London high-rise, or hangs low and full like a ripe tangerine over a harvested Indonesian rice field, the cycle of the moon's shadow silently echoes the rhythm of women's bodies. Like the ebb and flow of the rising tide, women's cycles of fertility wax and wane with the phases of the moon. That women are allied to this powerful force of nature is recognized in different ways all over the world - through moon goddesses like the Mayan IxChel or Greek Artemis from whom worshippers seek

affirmation of their powers to give birth, or simply through the words used to describe our reproductive cycles; the word menstruation itself comes from the Old English *mona*, which means moon. When our 'moon disappears', as the Mixtecan Indian women of Southern Mexico say, we suspect that we're pregnant.

Archaeologists excavating Palaeolithic sites in Europe have found bones marked with twenty-eight units, which they believe may have been used by women, tens of thousands of years ago, as primitive menstrual calendars. Women of the Chagga tribe of Uganda make notches on bark to mark the passing of their moons, and use the same system to calculate the development of their babies *in utero*. Amongst the Manus of New Guinea, little bundles of sticks are kept as moon counters; when ten bundles have been put aside, the baby is ready to be born.

When will my baby come? 266 days is the average time from conception to full term, although it may be as long as 300 days or as short as 240. Rarely do babies arrive 'on time'- for example, only 4 per cent of American babies are born exactly on the day predicted.

SIGNS

But we can't always rely on counting the moons to tell us that we're pregnant. A woman who's still breastfeeding a young child may not have begun menstruating since she last gave birth; a woman living in a region where periodic drought is a fact of life might miss the occasional period when her body is inadequately nourished. Even if our cycles are predictable, we look for signs.

In Jamaica, women know how to look for signs in their dreams: dreams of ripe fruit or shoals of fish mean they're pregnant. The Ancient Egyptians had a curious method for determining pregnancy. A potion of ground watermelon mixed with milk from a woman who had given birth to a boy was drunk or injected into the vulva. If the woman vomited, she was most surely pregnant!

The most common early sign of pregnancy mentioned by women in most cultures is a feeling of nausea, or morning sickness. Tribal women in Orissa, India, report a sensation of smelling something fishy, which makes them vomit.

Because of the same hormonal changes that can cause nausea, parts of the body darken early in pregnancy. Negrito women in the Philippines look for darkening skin in their armpits, in the backs of their knees and elbows, and sometimes on the belly, groin and thighs.

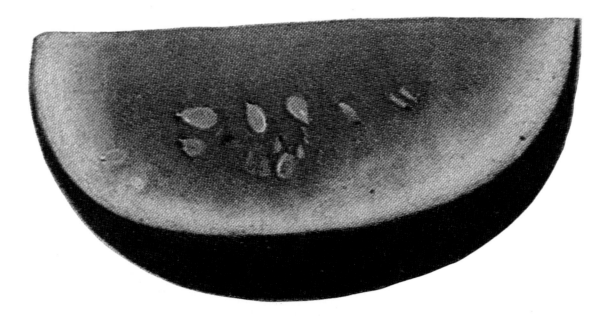

FETAL DEVELOPMENT

MOON OF THE FIFTH MONTH CASTS
ITS SHADOW
THE SECRET LIFE STIRS WITHIN ME
O MY DARLING, I CAN HEAR YOUR
HEARTBEATS.
(Indian birth song)

As the moons pass and bellies begin to bulge in odd places, a powerful need grows to know something about the hidden beings that implant themselves within us, to be born from our bodies and live with us as our children. What does it look like? What is it doing? What kind of metamorphosis is it going through, and how are we contributing to its growth?

Our drive to visualize uterine life inspired the extraordinary photographs taken by Lenart Nielson in the 1970s of embryos and fetuses living in their mothers' wombs. These images of the strange beings who inhabit our bodies are as fantastic and unearthly as the mental images of fetal development that people everywhere have always invented - as fantastic as the image a Lepcha woman in the Himalayas holds at the end of her first month of pregnancy, when she imagines in her womb a life form that is simply a pair of eyes.

The Chagga of Uganda say that during a woman's first months of pregnancy her baby undergoes a metamorphosis - not from embryo to fetus, but from a little worm, to a chrysalis in its cocoon, to a butterfly from which at four months a neck, head, and little arm and leg stumps begin. All this happens, Chagga women are told, because the mother's fountain of blood stops flowing to the outside world after conception, and builds the child in layers.

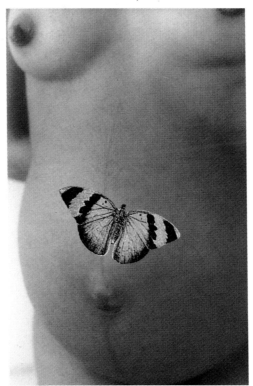

Nausea is caused by the higher level of oestrogen in the system, which causes irritation in the stomach as acids accumulate. Another reason for nausea is the rapid expansion of the uterus. Early morning is worst because stomach acids have accumulated and blood sugar is low after hours without food.

31

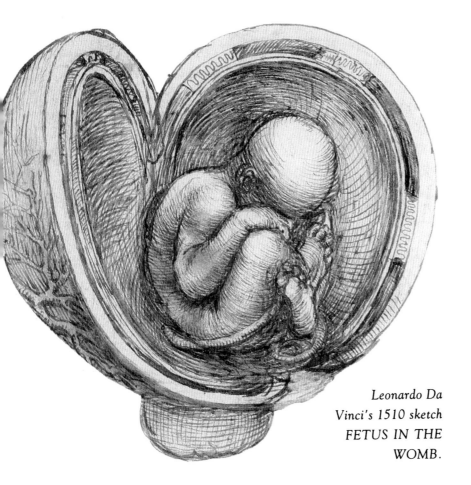

Leonardo Da Vinci's 1510 sketch FETUS IN THE WOMB.

Fetuses do indeed see, hear, touch their faces, yawn, stretch, hiccup and even exercise. The fetus also sleeps, maybe dreams - of what, we can only guess.

BIRD IN A NET BAG

When we imagine the beings growing inside us we're reminded that not only we, but our babies too, are preparing for the day of birth whether by nestling into a head-down position or, as the Azande of Africa believe, by fighting their way out of the placenta. They say that after the child is fully formed, toes and all, the mother's blood creates a little net bag in her belly for the child to live and grow in. When we feel something pushing out against our bellies, it's the child nibbling with its lips and pushing with its nose, trying to get out of the net bag. It finally makes a hole big enough to get its legs out and starts twisting and turning - that's what we feel just a few days before birth.

A Javanese woman believes that the baby inside her womb is, like a mystic in his cave, going without food and sleep while it meditates, strengthening itself spiritually for its emergence into the disturbing outside world. The Seri Indians of Mexico, too, say that in the last few months of pregnancy our babies are sitting calmly inside our bellies, holding their placentas in their laps.

HOW DOES YOUR BABY GROW?

It starts with a single cell which slowly becomes an embryo as it divides, again and again. By the beginning of the second month - just around the time you might be ready for a pregnancy test - the embryo looks like a little tiny fish, a quarter of an inch long, with a spinal column 'tail' that curls around to touch the head. In the third month the embryo becomes a fetus, as cartilage turns to bone and features grow more refined. The eyelids are completed, and close over the eyes. By the end of the fourth month (the first trimester) the fetus can fit neatly into the palm of your hand.

As the second trimester of pregnancy begins, your baby is almost complete, though still tiny and undeveloped. It might suck on its tiny thumb, which already has a membrane over its tip where the nail will emerge. Unique fingerprint whorls appear, distinguishing your baby from the other 4.6 billion people living on earth. If you listen through the stethoscope during the fifth month, you can hear your baby's heartbeat, and it can hear the rhythm of your heart as well as loud noises from the world outside. Nipples and eyelashes form. As the weeks pass your red, wrinkly-skinned baby starts doing gymnastics in your belly. In the eighth month it opens its eyes again, ready to meet the world. Soon, its nest becomes too cramped for it to do much in the way of gymnastics. Quietly it sleeps, feeds, and waits. In the short space of nine months a single cell hardly the weight of a dust speck will become a multi-million-celled baby, weighing on average seven pounds.

PREDICTIONS

WHO CAN TELL WHAT FISH IS IN THE
DEEP WATER?
WHEN THEY CATCH IT, WE SHALL
KNOW IF IT IS SAUR OR KOTRI.
MOON OF THE SIXTH MONTH CASTS
ITS SHADOW.
(From an Indian pregnancy song)

As the baby starts to turn, to kick, to hiccup inside the belly, we start to wonder more and more about its identity. Who is this person? Is it a boy or a girl?

If people ask me when I began to dance I reply, 'In my mother's womb, probably as a result of the champagne and oysters she ate - the food of Aphrodite.' (Isadora Duncan)

Most cultures have at least one method of satisfying a parent's hunger to know. Hungarian gypsies traditionally put a golden ring on the end of a string and hold it over the mother's belly. If the string swings in a circle it's a girl, if it swings back and forth it's a boy. Mormons in the United States say that if you have a bad complexion during pregnancy you're carrying a girl, who is taking beauty from her mother.

People in many parts of the world make right-left distinctions to say whether the baby in the womb is male or female. These superstitions are all based on an ancient scientific theory, developed first by the Ancient Greeks and adopted by medieval Islam and Europe, which says that females develop on the cool, left side of the uterus and males on the warmer right. The English used to make right-left predictions too, but as more and more women have amniocentesis or sonograms (medical tests which incidentally identify the sex of the baby) during pregnancy, the gender mystery is disappearing from industrialized society, along with a rich array of omens.

IT'S A GIRL		IT'S A BOY
Baby sits on the left side of the womb	Nyinba, Nepal	Baby sits on the right side of the womb
You put your left foot first crossing the threshold	Bihar, India	You put your right foot first crossing the threshold
Your left eye is brighter and your left breast bigger	Hippocrates	Your right eye is brighter and your right breast bigger
Baby sits low in the belly	Lepchas, Himalayas & Bedouin Tribes	Baby sits high in the belly
Baby sits high in the belly	Ancient Egypt	Baby sits low in the belly
If you're grumpy with women	Dinka, Africa	If you're grumpy with men
Fetus moves slow and gentle	Dusin, North Borneo & Egypt	Fetus moves fast and rough
If you first feel baby move when you're outside	Serbs, Yugoslavia	If you first feel baby move when you're at home
Dreams of human skulls	Maori, New Zealand	Dreams of *huisa* feathers
Dreams of prayer beads, necklaces, round parsnips	Nyinba, Nepal	Dreams of long radishes, aubergine, cutting tool
Dream of a headkerchief	Egypt	Dream of a handkerchief
Cravings for spicy foods	Nyinba, Nepal	Cravings for bland foods
Mother has red, fat cheeks	Nyinba, Nepal	Mother has thin, white face
Mother's face has yellow spots	Poland	Mother looks well
Belly is long	India	Nipples are black
Baby 'plays in stomach' before sixth month	Nyinba, Nepal	Baby 'plays in stomach' after sixth month

MORNING SICKNESS

Remedies for treating morning sickness abound, even though it usually subsides on its own before the fourth month as hormones stabilize.

REMEDIES PAST:

Ancient Rome - A drink of lime juice and water in cinnamon every morning.

Medieval England - Grains of Paradise (rare spice grown in West Africa).

Elizabethan England - Syrup of pomegranates, musk, lignum, aloes, cinnamon and sorrel, in water.

Eighteenth and Nineteenth-century England - Infusions of spearmint; for severe cases tincture of opium in mint, rose or cinnammon water; belladonna.

Europe & USA, 1960s - Thalidomide (Dostabal), later found to cause severe birth defects.

REMEDIES PRESENT:

Europe & USA, 1990s - Bicarbonate of soda, ginger ale, vitamin B6, frequent snacks of dry biscuits and nuts, especially before getting up in the morning.

China - Ginseng, fresh bamboo shoots, dried orange peel, ginger, liquorice root, and Grains of Paradise.

Hawaii - Ginger tea.

Jamaica - Fever-grass with rum, or straight for headaches.

Japan - Umeboshi plum.

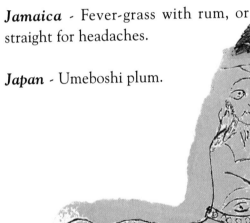

PROTECTIONS
AND PRECAUTIONS

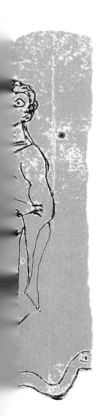

The French used to say of a woman who was pregnant that she was 'on the threshold'; the Ancient Chinese described her as 'the woman with happiness inside her'. All over the world, pregnancy is seen as a transitional stage in life, a time of transformation. The person who is suspended between two life stages is considered to be in a very vulnerable state, whether it's because she is dangerously close to the powerful world of spirits, or because she is biologically unsettled.

We're all aware that the substances we take into our bodies can affect the child; in the Himalayas, the Lepcha mother is told not to eat the rice stuck to the bottom of the cooking pot or the placenta might stick, just as we know to avoid substances like aspirin which can affect the flow of oxygen to the baby, or aerosol sprays, since the fumes could be harmful to the developing fetus. Tibetan folklore cautions a pregnant woman to avoid the shadow of the horse because she could become pregnant for as long as a horse is pregnant - twelve months.

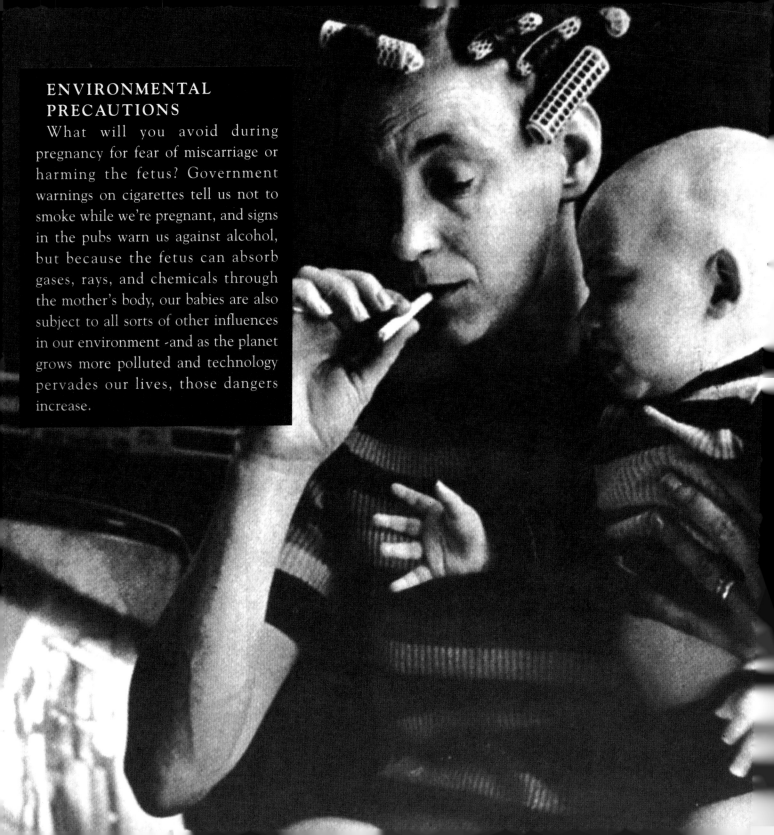

ENVIRONMENTAL PRECAUTIONS

What will you avoid during pregnancy for fear of miscarriage or harming the fetus? Government warnings on cigarettes tell us not to smoke while we're pregnant, and signs in the pubs warn us against alcohol, but because the fetus can absorb gases, rays, and chemicals through the mother's body, our babies are also subject to all sorts of other influences in our environment -and as the planet grows more polluted and technology pervades our lives, those dangers increase.

Doctors now advise mothers-to-be to avoid these potential risks:

INDUSTRIALIZED COUNTRIES

- CARBON MONOXIDE - Inhaling car pollution.
- INORGANIC LEAD - Dyeing your hair with chemically based dyes. Using lead-containing eye cosmetics. Breathing in lead paint fumes.
- ALUMINIUM - Cooking with aluminium pots and pans.
- BENZENE, TOLUENE, ANILINE, CHLORINE - Cleaning the house with heavy duty chemical products.
- CRESOL - Breathing in fumes from cleaning fluids and disinfectants.
- BIOCIDES - Spraying your house or garden with insecticides or pesticides (dioxin and chlorine).
- Working in places (like factories) with excessive noise, vibration, or heat.
- VINYL CHLORIDE PVC - Leaving the top off your typing correction fluid.
- X-RAYS - Exposing yourself to X-rays (including dental).
- ORGANIC MERCURY - Mercury amalgam fillings for your teeth.

NON-INDUSTRIALIZED COUNTRIES' PRECAUTIONS

- Lying too long in the sun will cause the fetus to melt away - Ibo, Nigeria.
- Eating hot food or drinking hot water can scald the fetus - East Africa.
- Sitting in front of the door can cause baby to have a big mouth and make a lot of noise - Java, Indonesia.
- Sleeping in the fields at night: a jealous ghost might steal your baby and you will bear a ghost child - Nyinba, Nepal.
- Gazing at an eclipse of the moon can cause baby to be born with a harelip - Aztecs, Mexico.
- Sleeping on your back can make the umbilical cord coil round the fetus - Bariba, People's Republic of Benin.
- Hanging the washing can cause the umbilical cord to get knotted - Navaho Indians, United States.

Many taboos are based on the idea of psychic imprinting: the baby, being of the same flesh and blood as the mother, is like a magnet recording her sensations as marks on the body or the personality. The intimate connection between a mother and her child is brought to life, and the deformities with which babies are born are explained. Several European and North American folk sayings reflect this idea - if you eat too many strawberries during pregnancy, for instance, your baby will be born with a strawberry mark on its body. The Gabbra nomads of northeastern Kenya believe that a pregnant mother should not watch videos, since the baby might become as strange and unusual as the fantastical images on the screen.

Precautions and protections reflect the fears that women everywhere share during pregnancy, new fears that only a mother experiences. Will my baby be whole and healthy? Will my baby come out too soon, before it's ready? Will it come out when it's time, or will it be stuck inside me? Protections and precautions function as insurance against harm. In the West today the list of things to be avoided and the things that can protect life is constantly growing, as society enters a new age and researchers discover the risks involved in various new environmental and body pollutants. A few people are beginning to question scientific thinking - avoiding sonograms, for instance, for fear that the baby might be harmed. And some, by wearing amber on their pregnant bodies or saying protective mantras, are looking for assurance back and beyond modern thinking to a world untouched by science.

SEX AND PREGNANCY

The relationship between a woman and her partner can change deeply during pregnancy. A new person has been added to the configuration, and nothing seems to highlight this fact more than the question of how the act of physical love relates to the child growing in the womb. Women feel differently about their bodies and men can feel differently about them too as the vagina becomes the birth passage, and breasts swell in preparation for the child. Some women feel more sensual in their pregnant bodies; others don't.

Many women feel that the openness and relaxation that come with lovemaking can help in the birth process. Orgasm stimulates and exercises the muscles of the uterus, use of the pelvic muscles keeps them supple, loving attention to nipples prepares them for breastfeeding.

But men and women in many cultures believe that they must abstain from sexual intercourse during pregnancy for fear of miscarriage or harming the child, especially after the first five months, when the baby can be felt kicking in response to the man's penis. A ruling of the Christian Church in the first century AD declared that 'religious women' should be chaste for three months before birth.

Nowadays Western couples are told that lovemaking with penetration can be harmful only when there's a danger of miscarriage or premature labour, particularly in the last six weeks before birth, because the oxytocin hormone released in orgasm is the same hormone that starts contractions. The Chagga of Uganda say a couple should take care in the last months and reduce lovemaking from ten to three times a day! But among the Kaluli of New Guinea, sex during pregnancy is essential because the man's semen is necessary to the proper development of the fetus.

We don't like to make love when we're pregnant. It will break the child and cause problems, but some people do if they like. (Scherzoom, a Nyinba woman in Humla, Nepal)

Of course we make love when we're pregnant! Without love, how can you get through life? (Panna Lal Datta, of the Santhal tribe, India)

43

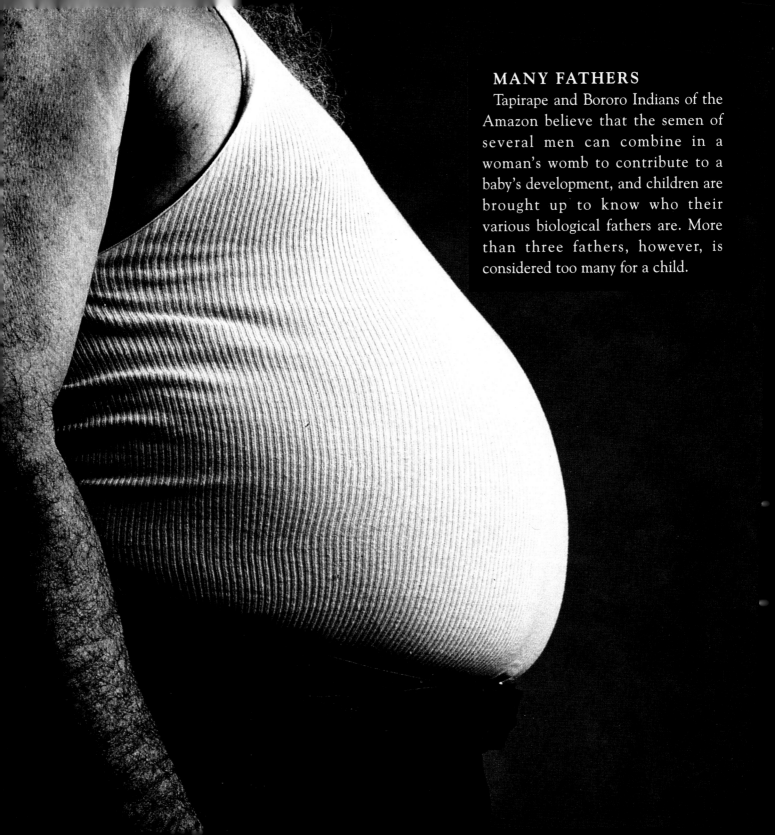

MANY FATHERS

Tapirape and Bororo Indians of the Amazon believe that the semen of several men can combine in a woman's womb to contribute to a baby's development, and children are brought up to know who their various biological fathers are. More than three fathers, however, is considered too many for a child.

PAPATOTO

How can you include your partner in pregnancy? Among certain tribes in South America and southern India, fathers must be on strict diets during their partner's pregnancy, lest they affect the fetus. Many societies recognize the father-to-be as a person in a state of becoming, whose intimate involvement is crucial to the well-being of the developing fetus. He might, like the Arapesh man, have to 'grow' the child in the womb by having sex with his partner as often as possible. He may be responsible for protecting his unborn child by providing the mother-to-be with all the food she craves - instead of rushing out for a pint of ice cream, a Sri Lankan father provides his wife with spicy green mangoes.

A man's emotions may be forgotten during pregnancy and the transition to fatherhood neglected to such an extent that many fathers suffer from 'sympathy symptoms'. Expectant Jivaro fathers of Ecuador recline in the house during pregnancy, coddling, dieting, and pampering themselves. In one English city 57 per cent of a group of 221 men whose wives were pregnant developed symptoms ranging from backache and toothache to abdominal swelling and an odd feeling that the baby was moving inside them, all of which disappeared once the baby was born.

Expectant Chagga fathers are taken aside and taught by the community of elders how to treat a pregnant wife specially, for fathers are responsible for creating a calm atmosphere. The elders sing, 'Well, my son, now you shall know what it is that a child kills in its mother's womb. It is you, and your boyish, youthful anger. If your wife makes you angry while she is pregnant, go over to the neighbour's and scatter your anger there!'

A father's day-to-day actions might be seen as affecting the baby. The Dyaks of Borneo are forbidden from violent acts like shooting a gun or sharpening a sharp instrument for concern that it will harm the growing fetus. Father and mother form a partnership in protecting their pregnancy and their child-to-be.

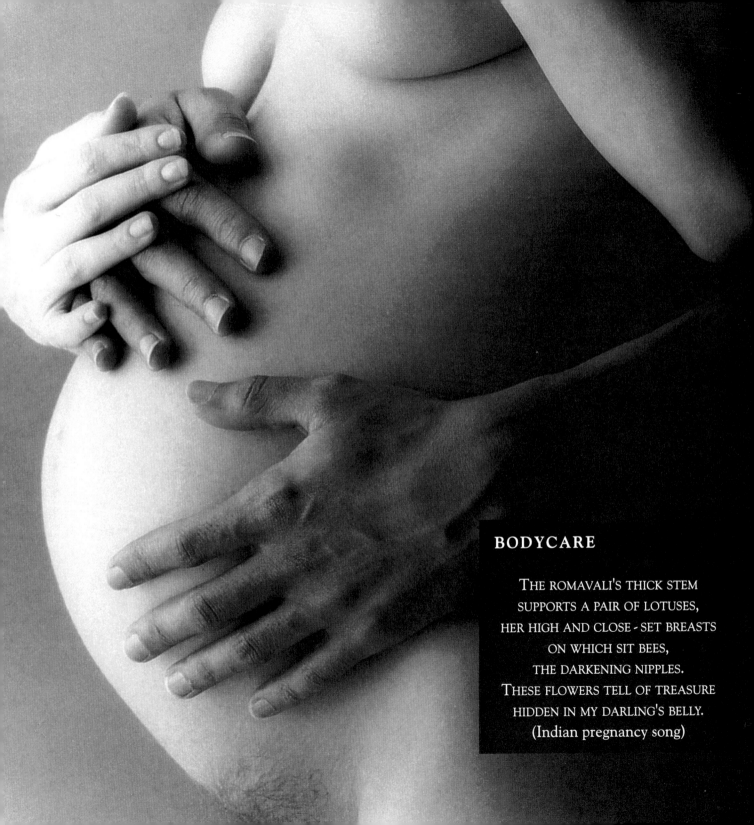

BODYCARE

THE ROMAVALI'S THICK STEM
SUPPORTS A PAIR OF LOTUSES,
HER HIGH AND CLOSE - SET BREASTS
ON WHICH SIT BEES,
THE DARKENING NIPPLES.
THESE FLOWERS TELL OF TREASURE
HIDDEN IN MY DARLING'S BELLY.
(Indian pregnancy song)

As a woman cares for herself, she becomes more in tune with her body. She can watch her breasts grow day by day as the swelling of her belly rises higher and higher, proof that the baby is growing inside. She can see the dark line moving up from the pubic region and down from the top of her abdomen. When it meets at her navel, say Hawaiian women, the baby is almost ready to be born. If she massages her nipples to prepare them for breastfeeding, as women in many parts of the world do, she might find some milky cholostrum leaking out - the baby's first food. All these signs help us to feel sure of the invisible life within. As this life within grows, our body undergoes rapid changes, stretching in pre-paration for delivery.

How we feel about ourselves during pregnancy has a lot to do with how we care for ourselves - whether, like women in most traditional cultures, we see beauty in our full bodies and so take the time to oil our skin and to scent our hair. Perhaps the way we care for our own bodies can prepare us for motherhood too, because in looking after our bodies we are, in a sense, mothering ourselves.

A woman's skin, which has to stretch during pregnancy and tends to dry and crack, needs special attention, just as the baby's skin will need its mother's loving care in the months to come. Every culture has its own preparation for skin care, traditionally made from the plants that grow nearby. A Hawaiian wo-man has warm kukui oil rubbed all over her body daily to lessen skin irritation and so reduce cracking. North American Indian women have the cut end of boiled rubber plant leaves rubbed directly on to their bellies and backs; the slippery juice is said to condition the skin and prevent stretch marks. Samoan wo-men have their bodies massaged with cocoa butter, Nepalese women use mustard oil, and in Malaysia coconut oil is rubbed into a pregnant woman's skin to keep it supple and lubricated.

The Bare Skin Facts: The average woman has 17 square feet of skin when she is not pregnant. This stretches to an unbelievable 18.5 square feet by the ninth month of pregnancy!

BATHING

One of the first things a Haitian woman does when she knows she's pregnant is to go to one of the older women in her family, who will give her special herbs for three magically protective baths to be taken in the next three days. If she has had a previous miscarriage, the *vodun* priestess gives her another special 'medicine' for bathing her stomach and vagina, as a precaution against the werewolves that are said to eat children in the womb.

Many people, like the Kanuri of Bornu, believe that taking hot baths during pregnancy is good for both mother's and baby's health; Hawaiian women are told to sway the abdomen gently in the water, so that the baby will become loosened and not stick at birth. Ancient Aztecs relied heavily on therapeutic bathing, and sweatbaths were recommended for pregnant women and new mothers. Sometimes the midwife would come and massage an expectant mother in her sweatbath. This practice continues today amongst Indian women in the Guatemalan highlands.

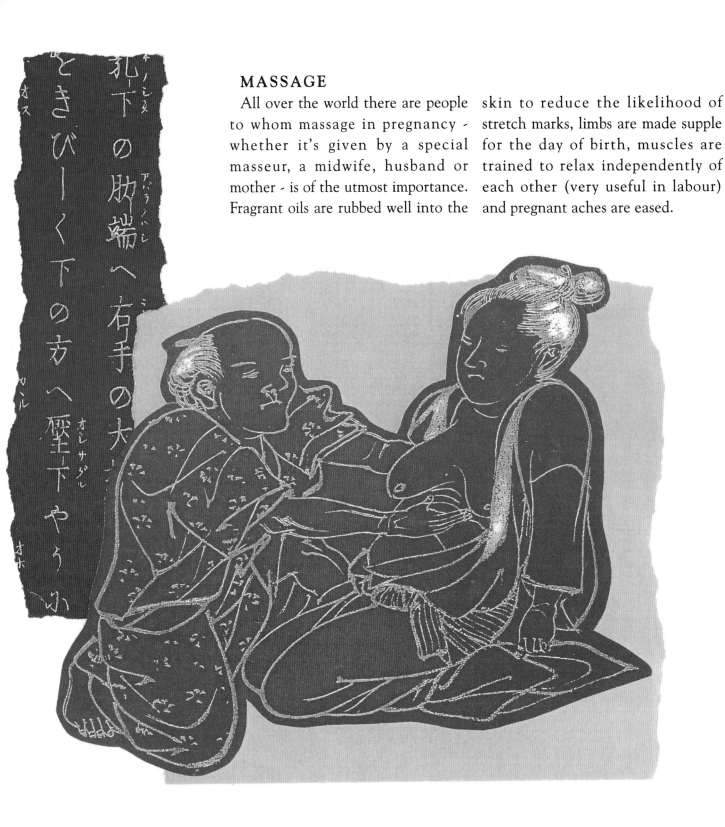

MASSAGE

All over the world there are people to whom massage in pregnancy - whether it's given by a special masseur, a midwife, husband or mother - is of the utmost importance. Fragrant oils are rubbed well into the skin to reduce the likelihood of stretch marks, limbs are made supple for the day of birth, muscles are trained to relax independently of each other (very useful in labour) and pregnant aches are eased.

BONDS OF TOUCH

The lower back is especially vulnerable to strain during the later months of pregnancy, as the muscles stretch and ligaments soften to support the growing uterus; massage of these areas can soothe pain and prevent damage to the muscles. Today, many Japanese women are massaged by their husbands during pregnancy using a form of shiatsu massage called *tai kyo*. Not only does massage help to bond parents together, but it can begin the bonding process with the child in the womb. The father stimulates the baby inside by pressing particular pressure points on the mother's belly. 'Jump up and down! Roll over! Somersault!' he instructs the fetus. Perhaps this custom encourages the infant to recognize its father's voice as it does its mother's.

A Mayan Mexican woman is given an abdominal massage by the midwife as they chat about how she feels, how the baby is doing, when it might be born. The midwife, stroking oil or vaseline into the woman's belly, can feel from one visit to the next how the fetus is growing and in what position it's lying. Massage is a way of keeping in touch with the growing fetus, besides giving the expectant mother time to relax and feel at one with her body.

SHAPING THE BABY

Some people believe that massage affects the baby not only indirectly, through the mother's emotional state, but also directly as it lies there in the womb, feeling everything very intensely through its well-developed tactile sense. Jamaican midwives 'shape the baby' when they give women their regular abdominal massages with wild castor oil. The Japanese practise *hara* massage, a special massage of the belly believed to stimulate the fetus and encourage it to get into a head-down position for birth.

In many hospitals it is standard practice to perform a Caesarean if the baby is breech (poised to come into the world feet first instead of head first) but English and Mayan midwives used to turn breech babies by massaging them into place.

SENSUAL ALTERNATIVE

Massage can alleviate or avert many of the discomforts - including varicose veins, headaches, cramps, and indigestion - that we can all experience during pregnancy, and can help an expectant mother to feel more at home with her changing body. Massage can also be a sensual alternative to sexual intercourse in the advanced months of pregnancy, for both mother and father.

Exercise, breathing, and preparing the passageway: the Celtic Sheela-na-gig of the Church of St Mary and St David, Herefordshire, UK.

'SOPLE THE PRIVIE PLACE'

Western culture places great emphasis on the swelling belly and breasts as the areas of the body most vulnerable in pregnancy. Mayan mothers pay more attention to conditioning the perineum - the folds of skin behind the vagina - because it too will have to stretch as the baby's head crowns at birth. Four hundred years ago an English midwife, Jane Sharp, recommended the use of an ointment containing the greases of hen, duck and goose, plus olive and linseed oils and hollyhock, to 'sople the privie place'. Tribal American Indians used the moist inner part of prickly pear cactus leaves to make perineal tissues more elastic so that they wouldn't tear during labour. Midwives in Guatemala and many other places massage pure olive oil into the perineum.

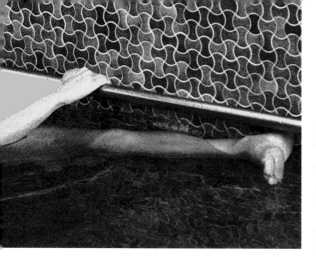

EXERCISE

Plutarch, writing almost two thousand years ago in Ancient Greece, advised that young girls should 'harden their bodies with exercise of running, wrestling, throwing the bar, and casting the dart', so that when they became pregnant their bodies would 'shoot out and spread the better', and would be ready for the strains of birth. Sanpoil women of India share this athletic approach to childbirth preparation. They embark on a special exercise programme during pregnancy, with a lot of running and swimming. Pregnant women in one New Guinea tribe climb over obstacles, and swim a few strokes while they're bathing.

BREATH OF STRENGTH

The Japanese take a more low-key approach. Women are introduced to certain breathing and posture exercises based on a theory of muscular control which says that if the ribcage is open, the pelvis will open too when the time comes to let the baby out. Zulu women of South Africa do breathing exercises not only in preparation for birth, but also to strengthen the child in the womb. Every morning the pregnant woman goes outside and takes three deep breaths in, then a long breath out to expel evil.

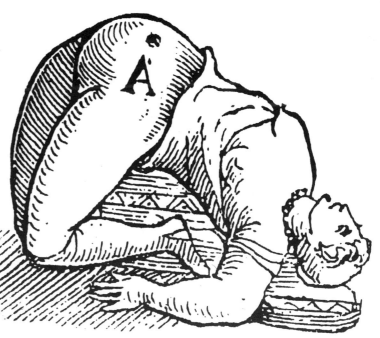

THE DRAWBACKS OF COMFORT

As Plutarch recognized, it's mainly in highly civilized societies - the worlds of labour-saving devices or slaves - that women need to condition their bodies for birth. The comforts of civilization can have their drawbacks in pregnancy, but exercise helps a woman who leads an otherwise sedentary life to feel good about her body, to become aware of muscles that have lain dormant for years, and to avoid some of the normal discomforts of pregnancy. We can also help ourselves just by becoming more aware of the way we use our bodies during our regular, daily activities.

THE EXERCISE OF DAILY LIFE

Many doctors and midwives today are telling us what Tonga women have said for years - that if you stay in one position for too long during pregnancy, either sitting or standing, your pregnancy will be uncomfortable and labour will be harder. Even if our work doesn't involve much physical activity, we can try walking rather than riding on the bus or climbing the stairs instead of using the lift. Consciously bending rather than stooping when we pick something up off the floor and stretching when we reach for a high shelf can help prepare our bodies for birth.

The hunter-gatherer Agta women of the Philippines hunt throughout their pregnancies, running after animals and shooting with knives or arrows, and carrying the meat back to camp. As Muhi Tudo said of Santhal women in her Bihar society, 'We need no extra exercise.'

One hundred years ago Western doctors used to believe that pregnant women risked miscarriage if they didn't rest their bodies, although in the more distant past, mothers in

medieval England were told to move around more than usual during pregnancy. Today, Western ideas have come full circle, and only the woman who is known to be at risk of miscarrying is advised to avoid strenuous activity. Only you can listen to your own body and recognize your own needs.

DANCE THE ACHES AWAY

Exercise doesn't have to be all work. Some cultures see dancing as a good way of preparing the body for birth - including the Hawaiians with their reclining hula or 'ohelo' dance, performed by men and women every morning. The *danse du ventre* ('womb dance'), otherwise known as bellydancing, is believed to have been practised not only as a rite through which the Mother Goddess was worshipped with pelvic rocking and rippling of abdominal 'birthing' muscles, but also as a form of gymnastic childbirth preparation.

From India to Ethiopia, dance can be a pleasurable form of exercise.

MIND CARE

If a mother fights with others while she is pregnant, the baby will come out fighting in childbirth, causing much pain. Later, the baby will grow up always fighting and arguing.
(Roogu, a mother of six, Humla, Nepal.)

In many cultures, people believe that as their babies develop in the womb, they are influenced by their mothers' experiences and state of mind. Nineteenth-century English mothers-to-be were advised to have a daily rest period in a quiet room where they could calm their emotions, lest, as the medical journal *The Lancet* said, the baby 'become imprinted with harsh passions or disfigurements'. The women of Humla take care to avoid any fights or quarrels, and even try to stay away from village gossip while they are carrying their unborn babies.

Women in Jamaica have traditionally believed that anything upsetting that the mother sees - such as a corpse - can upset the baby's development, and such things must therefore be avoided. Ibo women of Nigeria believe that if they're faced with a frightening sight they should put their hands over their navel so the baby won't see.

It might seem strange to think that the tiny being growing deep inside the belly can be affected by things that are going on in the world outside, yet we really know very little about what affects the unborn baby, or about the experience of being curled up in a bag of waters inside a woman's body. Taboos that regulate a pregnant woman's exposure to sadness or fright are based on a belief - only now gaining credence amongst Western scientists - that unborn children are influenced not just by the physical environment, but also by the emotional environment. In Western scientific terms this happens because hormones like adrenalin, released into the mother's bloodstream when she gets anxious, frightened, or angry, are absorbed by the baby's system too, irritating the fetus. Mexican Indians say that a mother's anxiety, which feels like knots in the stomach, can make knots form in the umbilical cord.

PAY ATTENTION TO THE PREGNANT WOMAN!
THERE IS NO ONE AS IMPORTANT AS SHE.
(Chagga saying, Uganda)

Amongst the Akamba in Africa, the whole community shares the responsibility of regulating the mother's experiences during pregnancy. In Bang Chan, Thailand, it's up to a woman to put herself in a cheerful mood while she's pregnant by looking at things that please her.

!Kung women believe that a pregnant woman should try to sit quietly and stay calm when her passions rise. As girls they're told that if they go through pregnancy fearing the day they will have to give birth, then both mother and baby might die in childbirth. Western medicine now believes that any kind of stress and anxiety during pregnancy can make labour more difficult - as if, the Nyinba say, 'the baby is fighting with you'.

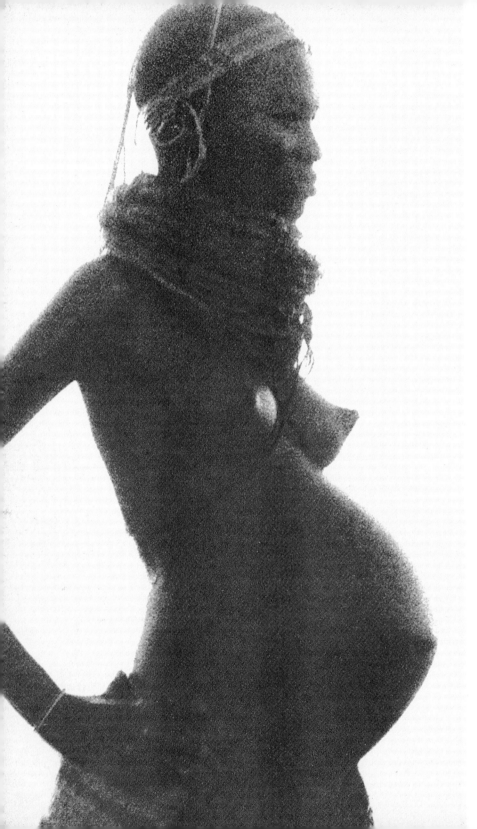

AWAITING BIRTH

MAY ALLAH GIVE ME A TRUE FRIEND,
WHETHER HE'S SMALL OR BIG,
LYING IN THE WOMB OR SUCKING AT
MY BREAST...
WHEN HE COMES FORTH WE'LL BE
FRIENDS.
ALLAH, GIVE ME A TRUE FRIEND,
WHETHER HE'S BIG OR SMALL.
(Nigerian song)

As the last months of pregnancy wind down towards birth and the body grows heavy, the belly uncomfortable, a woman becomes absorbed by private thoughts. She begins to think about birth. Nisa, a !Kung woman, said: 'When a baby is still inside you, before you give birth, you have many thoughts. You think, "The day I give birth, will I be courageous? Will I be afraid? Will I live? The day I feel the pains, will my heart be strong enough to withstand it?" '

During the seventh month of pregnancy, a Sudanese woman prepares ceremonially for the safe delivery of her child. Her hair is hennaed, braided and scented. She puts a special bracelet on her wrist for

A pregnant Turkana woman of Kenya contemplates the future.

protection and a knotted leather thong around her waist, and lies on a ceremonial wedding mat made of palm leaf stems, while her relatives gather round her. A special vitamin-rich porridge made from fermented millet is traditionally served. At one time the relatives would rub handfuls of this porridge - symbolic of regeneration and the life which will emerge - over the woman's swollen abdomen.

Pre-birth celebrations like this are both spiritual and psychological preparations for birth and parenthood. The community, too, is prepared to receive a new person into its midst. People come together - perhaps the families of husband and wife, whose unity will be vital to the new family; older people who can give seasoned advice; friends who will be the new parents' 'support group'. In North America it's customary for a woman's best friends to arrange a 'baby shower' for her during the last month of pregnancy. No prayers are said, but gifts are given for the baby - all the practical things it will need in its first few months of life - and advice is offered, based on the friends' own experiences of birth and motherhood.

The Mansi woman begins to prepare for her baby by building a small birch-bark cradle, in which her infant will sleep for the first week of its life. She also makes a small coverlet out of swan skin, and a pillow from a piece of deer fur twice the size of her palm. When these are ready, she sets to work weaving a mattress from bundles of long, dry grass, on which she will sit and sleep in the days following the birth of her child.

FACTS YOU DON'T WANT TO KNOW

SMOKING DURING PREGNANCY

THIRTY PER CENT OR MORE WOMEN IN THE USA, UK, CANADA, AUSTRALIA, NEW ZEALAND, AND NORWAY SMOKE DURING PREGNANCY. BETWEEN 1957 AND 1986 STUDIES OF OVER HALF A MILLION BIRTHS REPORTED THAT WOMEN WHO SMOKED DURING PREGNANCY HAD INFANTS OF LOWER BIRTH WEIGHTS (AVERAGING 200 GRAMS LESS) THAN WOMEN WHO DID NOT SMOKE. A FATHER WHO SMOKES TWENTY CIGARETTES A DAY WHILE HIS PARTNER IS PREGNANT IS CUTTING HIS BABY'S BIRTH WEIGHT DOWN BY A QUARTER OF A POUND. THE CAMPAIGN AGAINST SMOKING HAS MEANT THAT MANY SMOKERS SPEND THEIR PREGNANCY IN A STATE OF GUILT. MORE THAN HALF OF SMOKING WOMEN WORRY ABOUT SMOKING DURING PREGNANCY, AND 10 PER CENT ACTUALLY SMOKE MORE HEAVILY DURING PREGNANCY DUE TO STRESS.

HOW CAN YOU GIVE UP SMOKING? TALK TO YOUR MIDWIFE, SEEK OUT SUPPORT.

Preparing the Nest

Birth is the climax of a long period of transition which we call pregnancy, when a woman becomes a mother and a fetus becomes a child. In just a few hours the mysterious life within becomes a real, breathing, crying baby - a son or daughter, a sister or brother. How we welcome our children into the world reflects our highest hopes and dreams for them.

In a sense birth is also the birth of a mother who, like the fetus, has been growing into her new self as her belly

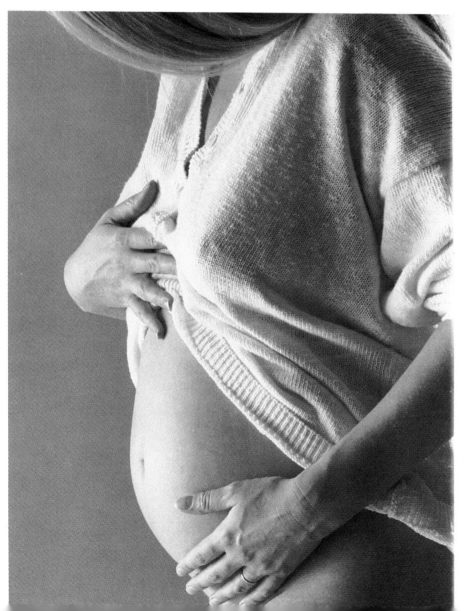

swelled. How do we want to become mothers? What kind of experience will this be for ourselves, our families and our babies? For a woman who is giving birth for the first time, and might give birth only once in her life, the events of these few hours and the choices she makes can have particular significance.

PREPARING THE NEST

As the day draws near when a woman will finally meet the baby she's been carrying inside her body for nine months, anticipation and excitement can make every little pang feel like the beginning of labour.

Then a day comes when the expectant mother is taken by a sudden urge to put things in order for the birth of her child. We know this as the 'nesting instinct', a sure sign that birth will be soon. The weariness of the past month gives

way to a flurry of activity as a woman on the verge of motherhood prepares a place in which to deliver and meet her child.

A woman in Bang Chan, Thailand, strings holy thread round the house walls from which she hangs cloths inscribed with magical letters and drawings. In many cultures, such as the Tanala of Madagascar, preparing the house involves stuffing every opening with rags or newspaper so that evil spirits will be shut out, and the birthplace will feel comfortingly safe.

What will you prepare for the day of birth? Perhaps you'll arrange the room in the home in which you plan to give birth or finally decide it's time to pack a suitcase for your hospital stay. You might think about the birthplace to which you're going, and pack a few special things to help you feel comfortable in a strange world.

The Mansi woman of Siberia, who goes to a birthing hut for labour and delivery, takes along her most beautiful kerchief to hang for the mythological woman who sends children.

WELCOME!

The Zulu of South Africa hang coloured beads and carvings round the birth room because they believe that it's very important for the baby to look on a thing of beauty in its first glance at this world. A woman who gives birth in a hospital will be returning home with a new person - perhaps you'll prepare the house and decorate around the baby's cot, so that its first experience of home will be pleasing. New babies are very sensual creatures - what will feel and smell good to the newborn? A Mbuti mother of Zaire goes out into the forest and looks for the most sweet-smelling vine she can find with which to make a cloth to wrap her baby. If possible, it should have a light-coloured bark which will look good against the baby's skin. She cuts the vine, beats the bark with elephant tusk until it's luxuriously soft, and paints swirling patterns on it with the juice of gardenia fruit.

Preparing the place of birth. Left: Macuna molucca paintings, Columbia. Right: Anuak village, Ethiopia.

HOME IS WHERE THE HEART IS

What kind of place do you want for your birth, and where should a child enter the world? In Egypt, the Sudan, and many other parts of the world, a woman returns to her parents' home, especially for a first birth, to be mothered by her own mother and to feel the protective warmth of a place in which she grew up. The Mbuti woman of Zaire gives birth wherever she happens to be when the time comes; probably it will be in the forest, her 'mother forest' to which she has introduced her unborn child, and with whose sounds it has already grown familiar.

What kinds of sights, sounds, smells do you want to be surrounded with during these hours when all your senses are in a heightened state? About 80 per cent of the world's babies - nearly all babies in non-industrial cultures - are born at home, in surroundings that are comfortingly familiar to the labouring woman.

BIRTHPLACE

Birth is a crucial episode in a woman's sexual cycle, and the place where we choose to open our bodies to another life can reflect that. Amongst the Dogon people of Mali, whose villages are laid out according to a complex scheme of sexual anatomy, women give birth in the central room or woman's domain, whose door symbolizes the female sexual organs and whose ceiling represents the man's outstretched body. Since the child was conceived in this room, it will be able to collect its life spirit here as it enters the world.

Where will you feel protected? In many parts of the world where birth is seen as polluting and threatening to the well-being of the household, a special birth hut is built, often round like the womb. The birth hut - or 'nest house', as it was traditionally called amongst the Maori of New Zealand - is an isolated, sacred space to which only certain people are admitted, and where women and their newborn infants are protected from the powerful spirits that gather around the mysterious events of childbirth.

As different options on where to have our babies become available, we can think about where we'll feel safe and at ease, and what we hope for most in our childbirth experiences.

Only a hundred years ago, women in England were strongly advised to have their babies at home for their own protection - during those pre-Pasteur days hospitals posed a serious threat of childbed fever. In the first half of this century women who chose to give birth at home in the USA were considered old-fashioned. By the 1950s birth was geared more towards hospital routines than towards the individual requirements of mother and baby. In 1965 a third of all births in the United Kingdom happened at home - by 1990, it was only one birth in a hundred.

'Home birth' can mean different things to different people. It can mean a bedroom, dimly lit and scented with myrrh; a sweatbath perched on a Guatemalan hillside, or a birthing pool in an English flat; a warm fireside in a Himalayan kitchen; the packed-snow sleeping platform of an Inuit igloo; or a one-room shack in Jamaica, with a washing line dividing the family bed and the children waiting on the other side for a first glance at the baby who will be held up for them to see. When a woman gives birth at home, she and her family have a degree of control over the event; it's their domain.

PRIVATE TIME OR PARTY TIME?

Who will be there at the birth of your child? The Hawaiians say that on the day of birth some women are seized with a longing to see a particular friend. If the person can't be there, a stone representing her is placed near the door so that the woman can feel her presence. They believe this means that the baby will be fond of that person. Since the bonds tying infants to the important people in their lives begin in the first minutes and hours after birth, it's possible that those present to meet the child as it enters the world will be the ones who bond most closely.

Some people see birth as a private experience between a woman and her baby. To the !Kung people of Botswana, the ideal birth begins in

In Holland, women educate themselves and make their own choices about birth; this gives them greater control over the experience. It is interesting that Holland boasts one of the lowest statistical rates in the world for episiotomy, the use of forceps, vacuum extraction and Caesarean section.

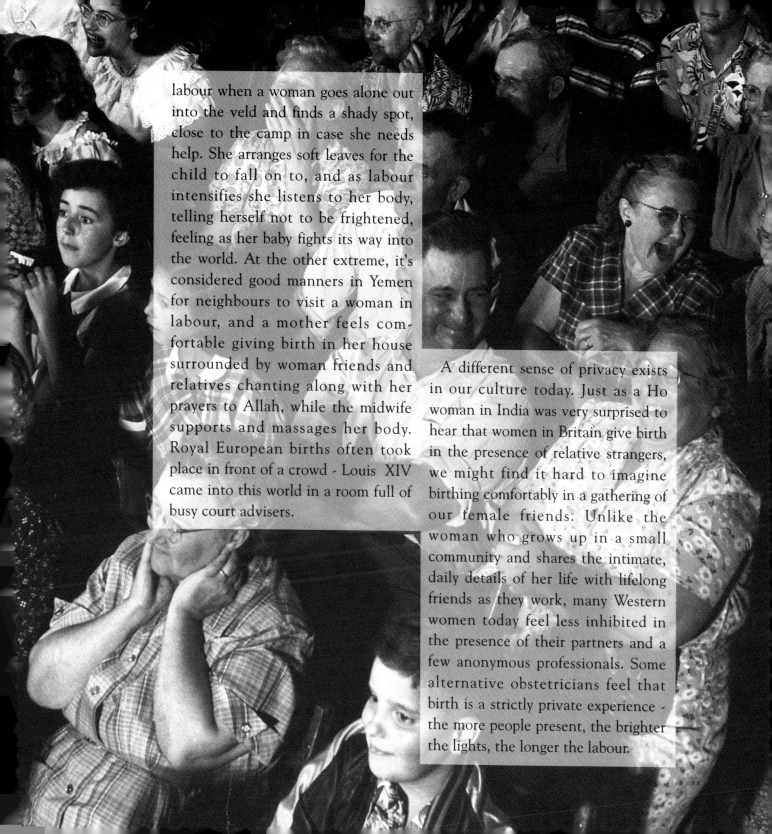

labour when a woman goes alone out into the veld and finds a shady spot, close to the camp in case she needs help. She arranges soft leaves for the child to fall on to, and as labour intensifies she listens to her body, telling herself not to be frightened, feeling as her baby fights its way into the world. At the other extreme, it's considered good manners in Yemen for neighbours to visit a woman in labour, and a mother feels comfortable giving birth in her house surrounded by woman friends and relatives chanting along with her prayers to Allah, while the midwife supports and massages her body. Royal European births often took place in front of a crowd - Louis XIV came into this world in a room full of busy court advisers.

A different sense of privacy exists in our culture today. Just as a Ho woman in India was very surprised to hear that women in Britain give birth in the presence of relative strangers, we might find it hard to imagine birthing comfortably in a gathering of our female friends. Unlike the woman who grows up in a small community and shares the intimate, daily details of her life with lifelong friends as they work, many Western women today feel less inhibited in the presence of their partners and a few anonymous professionals. Some alternative obstetricians feel that birth is a strictly private experience - the more people present, the brighter the lights, the longer the labour.

Fathers often care for children during mother's labour. Macuna father and child, Columbia.

FATHERS AT BIRTH

WHEREFORE AS THOU SEEST THAT THY WIFE ENDURETH TRAVAIL ON EVERY SIDE, THEREFORE THOU, O PARTNER, IF SHE FALLS INTO ANY NEED BE SURE THOU HELP HER TO BEAR THE PAIN ... FOR IT IS THY CHILD ALSO.

(St. Bernardino, fifteenth-century)

If giving birth is the culmination of becoming a mother, could helping his child be born be important to a man's progress to fatherhood? Perhaps it's no coincidence that as the number of fathers attending birth in Britain increased - a dramatic 53 per cent between 1974 and 1984 - men became far more involved in the day-to-day lives of their children.

What is a father's role during birth? In many cultures fathers are barred from the birth room; the father's job is to stand protectively close to the birth hut and pray for a safe outcome. 'Fight bravely like a warrior', begins the Chagga father's prayer for his labouring wife. If complications arise during birth, the worried Gabbra father of Kenya's role is symbolic - staying close outside the birthing hut, he will take off his belt

There are some women who like to have their babies with gravity instead of against it to please some obstetrician. (Margaret Mead)

He wants to interfere with his instruments, while I struggle with nature, with myself, with my child and with the meaning I put into it all, with my desire to give and to hold, to keep and to lose, to live and to die. (Anais Nin)

and trousers, releasing all constrictions to make way for an easier birth. Alternatively, in Bang Chan, Thailand, the father aids in the actual birth of his baby, so his hands may be the first to touch his child. He takes incense, flowers, and a lighted candle which will allow him access to the sacred world of the birth room. Then he prays for the winds of birth to come, for it is ultimately the wind, not he, that will deliver his child.

Tibetans believe that a long labour is caused by the father's presence - 'The baby is too shy to show its face to its father', said Urgyen, a mother of three children. Perhaps the shyness belongs to woman too. Only in cultures where men and women share their lives together intimately as partners - whether amongst some hunter-gatherers or in our own urban West - can they comfortably share in bringing their children into the world. Inuit men of the Arctic, for instance, deliver their own babies and help care for their children. Their nomadic way of life can't support extended families; couples live together in close quarters and there may not be a female relative nearby to help with birth or the new baby.

How will your partner participate in the birth of his child? What does he feel comfortable with?

SHARING THE PAIN

In medieval times, it was believed that pain could be transferred by the exchange of clothes. While a woman laboured in pain wearing her husband's garment, the father would be rolling on the ground, moaning and groaning in her dress as if it was he that was giving birth! This still occurs today in remote parts of Southern India, as fathers wear their wives' saris during birth. In Brazil, fathers will bleed themselves during their partner's labour, to share the pain of childbirth.

Among the Huichol Indians, the father traditionally sat above his labouring wife in the rafters of the hut, with a rope tied round his testicles. When his partner felt a painful contraction she would tug on the rope, so that he too would experience the pain which would bring new life.

It's the men that are discriminated against. They can't bear children.
(Golda Meir)

My grandmother was a midwife; she did it for all the family. She learnt it from her mother, and when I was a girl she let me watch ... The first baby I delivered by myself was when I was fourteen years old.
(Told to Fran Leeper Buss by Jesuita, a midwife in New Mexico)

MIDWIFE -
'SHE WHO HOLDS'

It's only recently that men have been accepted into the birth room in our culture. For thousands of years, midwifery was considered strictly woman's business, and if by chance a male physician was called to help, he had to dress up in drag and sneak into the birth room undetected. In 1646 a man was prosecuted for acting 'immorally' as a midwife.

The word 'midwif' simply means 'with woman'. The French call her 'wise woman'. The Germans know her as 'mother's adviser.' But to many people midwifery is a sacred and even magical craft; after all, what can be more important than helping to bring new life into the world?

In the Guatemalan highlands, women know from certain signs that God has chosen them for midwifery, and they learn the art from the spirits of dead midwives who appear in their dreams. In other cultures, midwifery is a craft passed down through the generations; as a girl, the Malaysian midwife-to-be attends births with her mother, who teaches her the art of massage and places her young hands on the labouring woman's belly so that she can learn to feel the position of the baby. Later she'll learn to perform birthtime's protective rituals - for instance, making sure that the labouring woman is aligned in harmony with the prevailing winds. Elsewhere, a midwife may simply be a woman of the community who, through her own experience, understands the special emotional and physical needs of a woman in labour.

In some cultures the midwife's main role is to support the labouring woman in her chosen birth position, standing, squatting, or kneeling; in parts of Ireland the term for midwife actually means 'knee-woman', and in Navaho society in the Southwestern USA, the birth attendant is 'she who holds'. As she supports the woman from behind, the midwife can massage her belly or back. In this position there's little else she can do besides giving verbal encouragement. It's the mother who actively controls and gives birth, while the midwife holds and soothes her with touch.

73

CALL THE SHAMAN !

Even where women still hold the responsibility for birthing their babies, a specialist may be called upon in the case of a very difficult labour. Rather than the flexible role of the midwife, who uses her own experience and intuition to follow a woman's rhythm in labour and give support when it's needed, the shaman's role is to bring magical or scientific knowledge to a situation that's no longer seen as 'normal'. It might be the shaman or medicine man who comes to chant a special chant, perhaps to prepare an amulet, or to call out the baby's spirit as the *bomoh* of Malaysia do. In medieval Europe it was the butcher or blacksmith who arrived with his tools in dire emergencies. And in the seventeenth century, with advances in obstetrical science, a new law ruled that a midwife had to call the doctor if labour wasn't progressing 'in due fashion'.

THE OBSTETRICIAN - HE WHO STANDS BEFORE?

The word obstetrics - meaning the science (as opposed to the art or craft) of midwifery - has its roots in 'to stand before'. But the role of obstetrics has been far from passive in modern Western birth. Some people argue that men, whether jealous of woman's power to give life from her own body or frightened by a powerful experience they couldn't understand, struggled to take control of the event, making woman a passive participant. Are the interventions of doctors - such as shaving a woman in early labour or putting her feet in stirrups - really necessary on medical grounds, or are they rituals designed to ease a man's fear of the unknown? Or was the struggle for control simply a struggle for professional standing?

Dr. William Cadogan wrote in 1748: 'It is with great Pleasure I see at last the Preservation of Children become the Care of Men of sense. In my opinion, this business has been too long fatally left to the management of Women, who cannot be supposed to have a proper knowledge to fit them for the Task, notwithstanding they look upon it to be their own Provence'.

It was the Queen of France's obstetrician who, in 1738, first

A man

introduced the practice of placing woman on her back in labour. The woman giving birth could no longer see her baby emerge, and had to push against gravity, but it was more convenient for the doctor. A little later, male doctors devised metal tools to pull the baby out, and as medical science progressed, doctors introduced labour drugs into the birth room. Drugged, women often have difficulty staying in tune with their bodies during labour and pushing the baby out, making them even more dependent on the doctor.

With doctors replacing midwives, pregnancy was increasingly seen as a 'condition' and treated as an illness rather than as a natural process of life. Midwives, once simply experienced and caring women, came under the rule of the medical establishment. With little knowledge of sterilization techniques, they often caused as much damage as intervening doctors by taking control of birth, and leaving women helpless to help themselves.

Male Helpers: from feared Man-mid-wives (usually butchers) to Victorian gynaecologists who plied their trade without looking.

BACK TO THE FUTURE

It's ironic that in an age where most Western women, because of better diet and health care, can more than ever before expect to have a safe birth and a healthy baby, childbirth is more than ever seen as a medical event belonging to doctors. Perhaps we're entering another transition in the birth room. As we gain confidence in our abilities to give birth without labour drugs and medical interventions, we have to listen again to the messages sent by our own bodies, and to rely on the kind of emotional and physical caring that midwives have traditionally given.

SIGNS OF LABOUR

MOON OF THE NINTH MONTH
CASTS ITS SHADOW.
HOW WEARY IS THE LIFE WITHIN;
WHEN IT SEES ITS DARK PRISON
IT STRUGGLES TO BE FREE
AND MAKE ITS CAMP ON EARTH.
(Indian delivery song)

Many first-time mothers wonder how they'll know when labour has really begun. We learn to time our contractions, which grow increasingly intense and rhythmic with labour. In the Southwestern United States, Indian women would drop stones as a way of timing their contractions. If the pulse beat six heartbeats - a beat for each breath labour had begun.

Those wretched babies don't come out until they are ready. (Queen Elizabeth II)

The first labour pain can be strong and definite - a sign, the Arapesh of New Guinea believe, of the baby turning over in the belly as it finally awakens from its long intrauterine sleep. After the first pain the strange, tightening feeling deep in the belly or back can come in waves, rising and subsiding and full of uncertainty.

Several other signs of labour's onset are recognized by women all over the world: a gush or steady trickle of fluids from the vagina, signalling the breaking of the amniotic sac; a pink-tinged discharge which means that the mucous plug blocking the cervix is dislodged. Malaysian midwives feel the woman's feet. If her big toe is cold, it means that blood has started to leave her extremities and travel to the uterus, warming it; birth will be soon. If her ankle is cold too, birth is imminent - for as the uterus heats up, the baby doesn't like it and wants to come out.

BORN WHEN IT'S RIPE

People in Tibet believe that whether or not labour is due, a child won't come out into the world unless the star under which it's destined to be born is shining. Western medicine has developed a way of starting labour artificially, by injecting into a woman's blood a simulation of the hormone oxytocin, which triggers contractions. For several years during this century, an unusual number of women laboured between the convenient hours of nine and five on weekdays.

Some women valued the implications of this control; uncertainty can make one anxious. In some cases induction can save lives. But often labour was induced just because a woman had passed her due date (although 80 per cent of American babies born 'late' are actually perfectly on time). The idea of hurrying the baby out for the sake of efficiency has lost a lot of its popularity in recent years - once there was a proper appraisal by women and medicine of the results of artificial induction on a mother's ability to cope with labour, and on fetal well-being. As the Malaysians say, a baby is like a fruit; it will be born when it's ripe.

Death and taxes and childbirth! There's never any convenient time for any of them!
(Scarlett O'Hara, in Margaret Mitchell's Gone With the Wind)

77

THE POWER OF WORDS

Vagina - The word vagina comes from the Latin *vaina* or *vagina* for 'sheath', the place where soldiers put their swords. In fact, in Roman times, Caesar would have been known for having many vaginas on his armour.

Jokingly applied to the female reproductive passage by Roman soldiers, the word has stayed with us.

HOW WAS JULIUS BORN?

Potential complications are a concern of every mother-to-be. Birth by Caesarean section is an ancient method, mentioned in the Talmud and, according to legend, the method by which Julius Caesar was born - hence the name. The first recorded modern European Caesarean was performed successfully in 1500 by a Swiss butcher.

Before the beginning of this century the risk of infection was too high to warrant surgical intervention in all but the most desperate situations. But after the 1950s, with hygienic machine-style hospital birth well established, the idea of lifting a baby out of its mother's abdomen without any unnecessary fuss started to take hold - what better way of ensuring a safe and painless birth! Many worried women were talked into the procedure when labour was taking its time, or complications arose (often as a result of labour being artificially induced); and of course, many were saved by it. By the 1980s, women in some parts of the USA stood a one in four chance of giving birth by Caesarean.

PENCILS AND TAILS

Penis - The word penis has an interesting origin. Penis originally meant tail, and only by extension was it used for 'male sex organ'. Penis (as in tail) later became a metaphor for brush, *peniculus* in Latin. As a result, etymologically, 'pencil' means 'little penis'.

Detail from an illuminated medieval manuscript of a woman surgeon performing a Caesarian.

HOW WILL YOU HELP YOURSELF DURING LABOUR?

Will you take sedatives to calm your fears and relax your body? Herbal remedies? A warm bath?

Will you try to dull the pain with analgesics? By relaxing and relying on your own body's secretion of hormonal painkillers?

Will you try local pain relief with regional anaesthetics, or with massage?

Will you listen to your body and breathe deeply into the centre of the pain?

Will you help yourself open up cervically by taking something to make contractions more intense? By visualizing your cervix opening, like a flower?

Will you listen to the rhythm of your body and help it along with music, or chanting?

FACTS YOU DON'T WANT TO KNOW

THE HORRORS OF THE STATE:
WHO OWNS MY BODY?

ROMANIA AND TIBET

WE TEND TO THINK OF OUR BODIES AS OUR OWN AND YET THERE ARE PARTS OF THE WORLD TODAY WHERE WOMEN'S REPRODUCTIVE RIGHTS ARE CONTROLLED BY THE STATE. IN ROMANIA UNDER CEAUSESCU'S REGIME, EVERY WOMAN, MARRIED OR NOT, WAS FORCED TO BREED, AND PRODUCE FIVE CHILDREN. SINCE CONTRACEPTIVES WERE UNAVAILABLE, AND THERE WAS OFTEN NO WAY TO PROVIDE FOR THE FIVE CHILDREN THEY WERE REQUIRED TO PRODUCE, THE SCARS OF FREQUENT ILLEGAL ABORTIONS (MANY WITHOUT PROPER ANAESTHETICS) HAVE LEFT ONLY 5 PER CENT OF BUCHAREST WOMEN OF CHILDBEARING AGE WITH HEALTHY UTERUSES.

TIBETANS TODAY SUFFER A CHILLING FORM OF GENOCIDE BY THE CHINESE, WHO HAVE FORCIBLY OCCUPIED THEIR COUNTRY SINCE 1950. TIBETAN WOMEN ARE CHECKED EACH MONTH FOR PREGNANCIES. ON EACH NEIGHBOURHOOD BLOCK IN THE CAPITAL, LHASA, A FEMALE GOVERNMENT OFFICIAL MONITORS MENSTRUAL CYCLES. ANY TIBETAN FEMALE DISCOVERED TO BE PREGNANT IS TAKEN TO THE HOSPITAL FOR AN ABORTION. BY THE END OF 1989, 87,000 WOMEN HAD BEEN STERILIZED IN QINGHAI PROVINCE IN CENTRAL ASIA. THE CHINESE GOVERNMENT'S TERRIFYING JUSTIFICATION OF THESE GENOCIDAL PRACTICES MAY BE FOUND IN ITS OFFICIAL REPORT ON FAMILY PLANNING POLICY: 'IT IS MUCH MORE COMMON TO FIND IN THEIR POPULATION PERSONS WHO ARE MENTALLY RETARDED, SHORT OF STATURE, DWARFS AND INSANE.' WHILE THE LEGACY OF CEAUSESCU'S BRUTAL REIGN LIVES ON IN THE THOUSANDS OF UNWANTED CHILDREN IN STATE ORPHANAGES AND THE SCARRED WOMEN FORCED TO BEAR THEM AGAINST THEIR WILL, TIBETANS WILL BE LUCKY TO HAVE CHILDREN OF THEIR OWN WHILE THE CHINESE CONTROL THEIR HOMELAND.

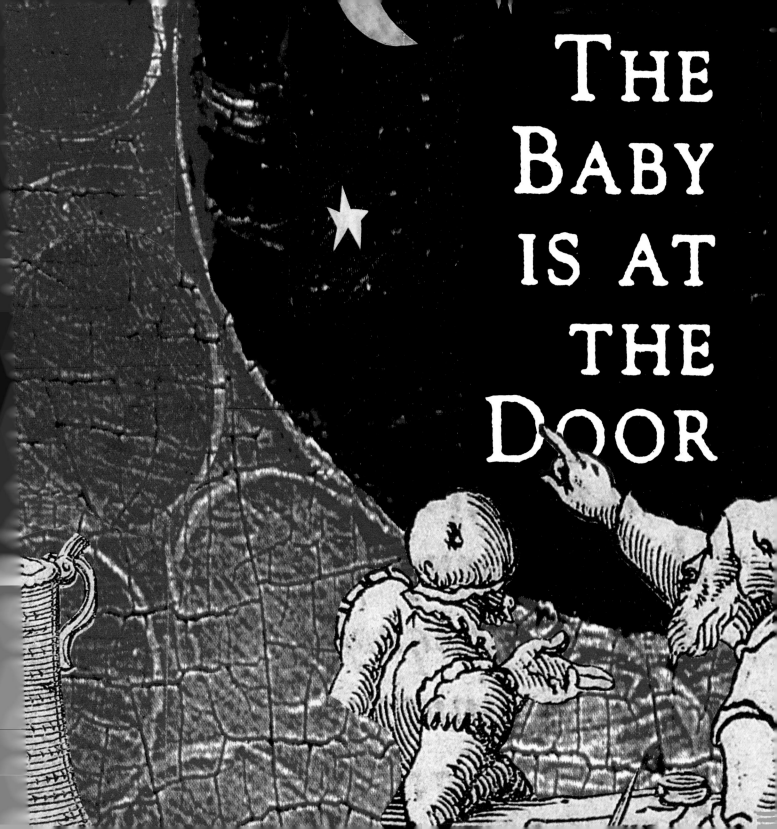

THE
BABY
IS AT
THE
DOOR

As labour contractions become rhythmic and increasingly intense, most women feel excited, and somewhat apprehensive. What will you do during this time to help labour along, and to relax until the midwife comes or as you wait to go to the hospital?

With amber and coral beads strung around her neck for luck, a Yemenite woman paces the floor intently, pausing to lean over during contractions. Western medicine has recently discovered that walking as much as possible

during the first stage of labour can make contractions much more effective. We probably knew this instinctively in centuries past; four hundred years ago in England a woman in early labour was advised to go up and down a pair of stairs, crying out as loudly as possible 'so to styre herself', and to sit down only when birth was imminent.

BEARING THE PAIN

ACTIVE LABOUR: THE FIRST STAGE
During the first stage of labour the cervical and uterine muscles are expanding and contracting to stretch the neck of the womb to its limit of about 10 cm. This stage can last from minutes to days. A first labour can usually last between eight and twelve hours.

Blessed chloroform. (Queen Victoria)

When Queen Victoria defied the Christian tradition of stoic labour and demanded chloroform to spare her the proverbial suffering, she triggered a century of research into new drugs for making labour a less painful experience. Doctors' medicines were by no means the first labour drugs - wherever herbs are gathered and used medicinally, people know some that are helpful in childbirth. But the results of modern chemical technology were far more dramatic, and women welcomed them eagerly. In the process, we forgot some of the ways in which a woman can help herself get comfortable in labour, and experience childbirth not as suffering but as giving forth life.

Alongside the development of chemical relief for labour, Western science has shown us the power of our own bodies to help us through childbirth. We know that as labour begins, our systems release their own supply of natural painkillers - morphine-like chemicals called endorphins. If we fight our sensations and tense up, we interfere with the secretion of these chemicals. Perhaps this is why !Kung bush-

women say that fear is what causes a woman and her child to suffer in childbirth.

WILL YOU SCREAM?

Will you try to be silent during your labour, like the Gabbra women of the Chalbi Desert, or will you scream, like women in the Sudan who believe that any attempt at courageous endurance will make them vulnerable to the evil eye?

Some alternative midwives believe that mouth and vulva are connected; just as the baby is going to come out, there's a powerful urge to let out a wide-open cry - like the cry of the Ainu women of Japan who call out for help from the 'little grand-mothers'. But many Western women feel embarrassed at the idea of crying out amongst strangers in a hospital, as do women in Hawaii or Uganda who learn that if they yell during labour they'll make themselves the talk of the neighbourhood. The choice is yours. You might see childbirth as a private experience between you and your baby, and let yourself scream, or, as Hopi Helen Sekaquaptewa suggests, 'Don't yell or scream. Keep the air in to help expel the baby'.

Oh, it hurts so much it is as if you have died, and only when the baby rubs your legs coming out, do you live again. (Habiba, a Gabbra mother)

Oh, I almost cried out in my in-laws' village. (Gabbra song)

TRANSITION: THE TIME OF DESPAIR

Wherever you may be, my little grandmothers, please help today a suffering woman! (Ainu birthing chant)

When the cervix is almost completely open, some women experience a phase known as transition. Your legs may tremble and cramp, you may vomit, you may want to push before you are fully dilated. The pattern of contractions will change as the womb gets ready to push the baby down. This can be the hardest part of labour, the time when you want to quit and go home: you've had enough.

COUNTING THE STARS

Malaysian women try to keep their minds on holy things as they feel themselves being swept away by the overwhelming sensations of labour, and women in our own past were encouraged to pray devoutly to God. Today, many couples from Europe to China and America work on altering the sensation of pain through the 'mind-over-body' Lamaze system of rehearsed breathing and relaxation techniques.

The Zulu woman of South Africa also practises special breathing exercises during pregnancy, and as her labour grows intense she concentrates hard on breathing alternately through her mouth and nose. Traditionally, above her head is a hole in the roof of her hut where, at night, the stars shine through. She tries to focus on this sky; this is why Zulu women say that in labour they are 'counting the stars with pain'.

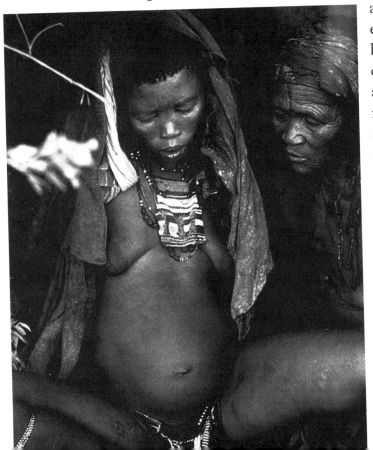

Wearing protective amulets, a !Kung San mother focuses inward during labour. Opposite page: Indian women imagine lotus petals unfolding to help the cervix open in this 17th century Italian engraving.

LISTEN

We can focus our attention away from our sensations, or we can try to flow with the contractions, focusing on them, quietly listening to our bodies and keeping in touch with what's going on inside us through breathing. We can breathe rhythmically and deep in our bellies, into the centre of the opening cervix.

LOW LIGHT AND QUIET

It's possible that a dimly lit, almost womblike space can help us to forget the distractions of the outside world and focus on the worlds within our bodies. As a Mayan woman's labour grows intense the friendly conversation that kept her relaxed in the early stages wanes, allowing her to enter her own peaceful, inner space.

PETALS UNFOLDING

We can also try to harmonize mind and body by creating mental pictures of the process taking place inside us. A woman in India helps herself by watching a lotus flower. As its petals gradually unfold, she can imagine her cervix opening with each contraction, making a passageway through which her baby can pass into the world.

Tab. IIII.

SOOTHING SOUNDS AND MOVEMENT

Amongst Navaho Indians, it's traditional to play music as a way of helping women tune in to the rhythm of contractions; perhaps, now that many hospitals allow tape recorders in the birth room, we could think about what kinds of music would help us to follow our natural rhythms. Similarly, in remote areas of Saudi Arabia a mother in the throes of labour is surrounded by women who perform belly dances around her, hypnotizing her with their rhythmic, rippling movements so that she too will move and breathe with, instead of against, her body.

SWIMMING WITH THE WAVES

When contractions start coming in mounting waves it can be very hard to swim over them, because all the muscles in the body tend to tighten in unison. How can you help your body to relax while the strongest muscle in it, the pregnant uterus, is contracting with more force than anything you've ever felt? Indian women of the Guatemalan highlands are massaged by midwives in a steambath; some

inadvertently give birth to their babies there because they're so relaxed.

Every woman experiences labour differently, and each labour is unique. You might need the stimulation of sounds, smells, or touch for a while and then quiet, internal peace. You might want to be touched, or left alone with your own body. You might find that you can help yourself with controlled breathing or by counting the stars, only to feel as if you need to let yourself slip away into a more instinctive state as the experience of labour changes from minute to minute and hour to hour.

PRE-BIRTH BATHING: WINDING DOWN WITH WATER

Nobody knows exactly why soaking in warm water feels so good in labour. Even the sight and sound of the water flowing can be enough to help a woman in labour open up. In the highlands of New Guinea, a Gahuku woman gives birth by the riverside, where she can watch the dark green of the water lapping up against the banks while other women bathe her back and shoulders with cloths dipped in the river. From the Soviet Union to Britain, the benefits of water as a means of helping the later stages of labour are increasingly recognized and utilized. In Britain about 1,000 women have given birth underwater in the last five years. Surrounded by water which cuts her off from outside noises, a labouring woman is able to focus her attention inside herself on the task at hand. Cervixes may dilate rapidly.

WATER BABIES

A few years ago scientists at the University of Copenhagen offered a group of women in their first stage of labour the choice of taking a warm tub bath. Half the women accepted the offer, and found that their cervixes dilated at twice the rate of women who stayed dry. They also used far less in the way of tranquillizing and contraction-stimulating drugs than the control group. In neighbouring Sweden, it's been found that a disproportionate number of children are born on Mondays, two days after the traditional Saturday sauna!

Over 1000 women in the UK have given birth in water since 1987.

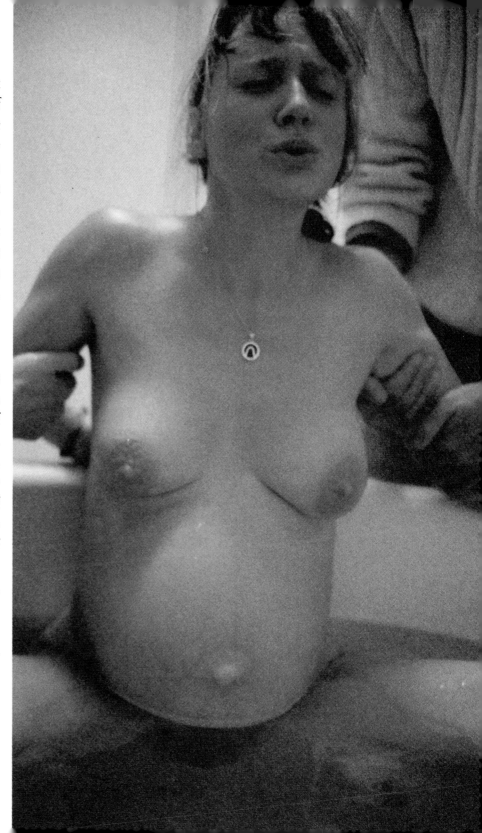

AROMATHERAPY IN LABOUR

As we tune in to our most instinctual selves during labour, our senses reach their highest level of receptivity - including our sense of smell. We know that since this sense is directly linked to our store of memories, it can affect our moods, but could different scents have the power to soothe or invigorate us during labour, or to alleviate the anxiety that makes it so hard to let go and flow with our contractions? Perhaps. Many people believe that the chemical properties of the fragrant oils found in flowers, leaves, roots and barks directly affect our nervous systems.

Women in some traditional cultures crush aromatic herbs in their hands and inhale the delicious fragrances as a way of easing labour. The scent, absorbed by nasal membranes, enters the bloodstream and alters the chemical balances in our bodies. The Romans liked to scent the birth room with lavender, a herb which gently stimulates while fighting muscle fatigue, while in the Sudan, incense is burned during labour. One of the most luxurious ways of inhaling the fragrant vapours is to put a few drops of essential oil into the bath while you soak away your labour tensions.

Three hundred years ago, English midwives used sweet-smelling oil of lilies for massage in labour. Fragrance and touch relax you while the oil, rubbed into your skin, enters your bloodstream and goes to work on organs and muscles. Another traditional method was fumigation - a seventeenth-century midwife suggested that the smoke of marigold flowers be 'taken in by a tunnel at the "secrets" ' to help in the expulsion of the placenta!

HEAT HEALS

Warmth in itself can help our bodies relax; when the body is cold, just as when the mind is fearful, excess amounts of adrenalin are produced which can interfere with the secretion of endorphins. In times past, the midwife would wrap women in sheepskin, letting them soak up their own body heat. Locally applied heat helps to ease the sensation of contractions. During a long and tiring labour a Jamaican midwife wraps the mother's belly in hot towels, then massages her all over with oil to stimulate circulation. If back pain is a problem, she pulls a strip of cotton from side to side across the woman's back for the warmth of the friction; the Ainu in Japan ease back pains with warm chips of elder. Several American Indian tribes used dry poultices of warm earth applied to a woman's belly, just as we might use a heating pad or hot-water bottle.

Heat heals an Azande mother in southern Sudan.

93

TOUCH

Let the midwife herself sit stooping before the labouring woman and let her anoint her hands with the oile of lillies and of sweet almonds and the grease of a hen mingled and tempered together. (Seventeenth-century English text on midwifery)

Most of all we can learn, or relearn, about the simple therapy of touch. Just as we will soothe our newborn infants by touching, caressing, stroking their bodies, we ourselves can have our stresses soothed with massage. All over the world women in labour have their legs, hips, bellies, breasts and backs massaged; Tentekara women in Brazil massage their abdomens themselves; many women instinctively stroke their own bellies during labour with a light, rhythmical, circular touch called *effleurage*.

MASSAGE

Malaysian mothers like to have their navels massaged with coconut oil - they say it helps the baby to descend. Japanese women like to have their leg muscles massaged during a difficult labour, for they believe that leg muscles are linked to muscles in the vagina and pelvic floor. If your leg muscles are relaxed, then your vaginal muscles will relax too and birth will be easier. Another traditional Japanese remedy for labour pains is to press on the side of the woman's little toe on each foot, at a shiatsu pressure point on the inside of her ankles, and on her sacrum.

The traditional Jamaican midwife has a whole repertoire of massages for different stages of birth. At the beginning, she massages the labouring woman's abdomen with the slimy part of toona leaves to make sure the baby gets into the right position; to help the contractions along she wraps the abdomen in hot towels and then rubs the woman's whole body lightly with olive oil; and to ease the intense pains that come before the pushing starts, she pats her belly with a warm, damp rag. Mayan women have their abdomens massaged by the midwife, who puts two fingers under the uterus and pulls it up towards her. Even an untrained massage can help. When you feel the comfort of having your body rubbed with fragrant oils, your mouth naturally relaxes - and as your mouth relaxes, so do you.

Be thou male or female, come forth, the saviour calls thee.
(Invocation from medieval England, written and tied above the woman's knee during a difficult birth.)

HASTENING BIRTH

Different cultures have different ideas about how long labour can safely last and what should be done if the cervix isn't opening to allow the baby's passage into the world that is awaiting its arrival. Jicarillo Indian women in Mexico might be in labour for three to four days before they are given special herbal 'medicines for birth'. In Yemen, a long labour can last up to a week. How do you, as Zulu women of South Africa say, help a child 'get through the road that is closed'? In a Western hospital the doctor is usually called in, and the mother might be given pitocin to stimulate stronger contractions so that the road will open more quickly. Indian tribal people of Central and South America have a large medicine chest of natural remedies for pregnancy and labour, including plants which stimulate a woman's secretion of the hormone oxytocin - the natural form of pitocin.

TWEAKING NIPPLES

Lepchas women of Sikkim, and the Siriono in Bolivia, find that nipple stimulation makes contractions stronger and more effective. This is because oxytocin is released not only during labour but also when a woman suckles her child and when she is sexually aroused. Perhaps there are a few answers here for fathers-to-be who feel left out of the physical process of birthing.

PEPPER AND EGGS?

Some of the strangest sounding methods have a practical basis for hastening a long and difficult labour. During the sixteenth-century English midwives would blow sneezing powder or pepper up a woman's nostrils if labour had been going on for a long time. Sneezing actually causes the diaphragm to press on the uterus, as does retching. Perhaps this explains why a Mayan midwife breaks two raw eggs directly into the mother's mouth.

RITUAL REMEDIES

When herbal medicine for a difficult labour is given to a Bariba woman in the People's Republic of Benin, the midwife immediately drops the container on the floor, just as everyone hopes that the child will drop. When we're anxious and exhausted, wondering whether we're really capable of giving birth, symbolically magical gestures like this can ease our anxieties by reminding us that eventually our bodies will open for our babies. In Chittagong, Pakistan, doors and windows are thrown open, all knots are untied, bottles are uncorked, cows and sheep are untethered. In Malaysia a woman's hair, tied back to keep her cool in labour, is let loose.

Many of the rituals practised during a difficult birth help a woman to visualize the things that have to happen in her body so that the baby can come out. Amongst the Cuna Indians in Panama a special chanter is called to release the baby from Muu, the goddess 'grandmother' who lives in the uterus as its prenatal mother and occasionally grows so attached to one of her babies that she refuses to release it from her house.

Seated below the labouring woman's hammock, the chanter sings an epic song describing the difficult journey of shaman spirits along subterranean rivers and paths to Muu's glorious house. The song culminates in an intense battle between the army of shamans and Muu. Finally, the shamans win, find the fetus and accompany it out of the birth canal four abreast!

OPENING THE HEART
TO OPEN THE BODY

ACTIVE
LABOUR:
THE SECOND
STAGE
Your cervix is wide
open and the
muscles in your
uterus and
abdomen start to
push the baby
through and down.
Your position
during this stage is
important in
easing delivery of
the baby.

There is much to be learned from other cultures about the psychology of birth - a subject that Western medicine is only now beginning to explore. In the Guatemalan highlands and several other societies where sin is seen as the cause of difficulties in labour, the mother is asked to confess to the midwife. Perhaps she broke a pregnancy taboo and is worrying that her baby might be affected; releasing her anxieties can help her to release her baby. If this doesn't work, the father is asked to confess. Perhaps the woman can't let go of her baby because she's unsure of her relationship with the child's father. Finally, if the baby still isn't coming, its father's loincloth is brought and tied round the woman's belly to help assure her that he'll be there for her and her baby.

We bring to our birth experiences all sorts of worries - not just about whether we'll really be able to give birth, but also about our changing bodies, our changing roles as women, and our changing relationships. Could it be that when we feel blocked psychologically, we become blocked physically? Subconsciously, we keep the baby inside, afraid of letting go because the minute we let go to allow a new life to enter the world, our new lives will begin too. Sometimes when labour is blocked it helps simply to talk these things out.

A woman releasing her baby into the world is, in a sense, doing something she will have to do time and again as her infant grows into a child, leaves her lap, and ventures away from her protective embrace. It can be hard for a mother to let go and share with society this life which has been so intimately and privately connected with her body. But, as the Hos magician proclaims when he is called to a long labour to unbind the baby in the womb, 'Today is the day for the bonds between this woman and her child to be cut'.

98

THE PUSHING WIND

Suddenly, when a woman's cervix has finally dilated so that it's wide enough to let her baby's head through, she feels the 'pushing wind', as it's called in Bang Chan. The urge to push the baby out comes as a relief to many women because now, finally, mother and baby can work together as a team. As a Mayan woman bears down, her friends and helpers might begin a steady, rhythmic chant of 'Haul! Haul!', reminding her that the action of moving the baby through the cervical opening is like the work of drawing water from the well.

How can we help ourselves and our babies during this second stage of labour? Whether a woman sits, kneels, squats, stands, gets down on all fours or lies on her back while she pushes her baby out has a lot to do with the culture in which she lives - how her mother gave birth to her, the images of childbirth with which she has grown up, the craft and technology of delivering a baby, even language itself. The French word for 'to give birth', *accoucher*, means 'to lie down'.

The uterine muscle, the largest muscle in the human body - larger than any muscle in a man's body and bigger than the biceps of a champion boxer - launches a baby into the world.

Childbirth can be a vulnerable time, full of emotional stress. This Balinese wood sculpture shows a leyek, a demon thought to frequent birthing rooms waiting for a chance to devour the newborn infant.

BIRTHING POSITIONS

Women in many parts of the world say that since every labour is different, every woman has to find the birthing position that suits her and her baby best.

CRESCENT MOON

Given the choice, many women intuitively adopt semi-upright positions like squatting or kneeling, in which the back curves like a crescent moon; this opens up the cervix so that the baby has an easier time negotiating the bones and muscles leading into the vagina. Perhaps we find these positions comforting because they're so flexible, letting us move with the baby and rock our pelvises when there's back pain.

SQUAT

It's only natural that women who squat every day to cook, eat, wash, plant and gather should feel comfortable squatting to give birth. But women who are used to the comfort of chairs find it hard to squat for any length of time unless they've practised during pregnancy.

HAMMOCKS

A Tapirape woman of Brazil lies in her string hammock with her legs hung over the sides and her back cradled in a gentle C-curve. A two-inch slit is cut in the hammock for the baby to be born through. When she feels the urge to bear down, she pulls on two wooden poles at each side of the hammock.

ROPES

In rural areas of the Sudan, traditional 'rope midwives' hang a rope from the ceiling for the mother to grasp and bear down on while she squats against a pillar.

BODY PHYSICS

Lepcha women of the Himalayas squat, leaning back against the warm bodies of their partners. The man supports the woman with his arms under hers, and massages her breasts and belly between contractions.

In Bang Chan, Thailand, a woman leans back against her husband's body while he digs his toes into her thighs; perhaps this toe pressure, like oriental shiatsu, gives her some relief.

FEET-TO-FEET
Some women of the Mbuti tribe in Zaire sit feet-to-feet with a friend, holding hands.

MOTHER'S LAP
In Tonga in the South Pacific, a woman in labour sits on her mother's lap on a floor specially covered in soft mats.

SLEEPING POSITION
Zuni women of the American Southwest once gave birth lying on their sides, facing the midwife. With each contraction, the woman would pull on the midwife's belt while another helper behind used the heel of her hand to put pressure on the mother's lower back. This counterpressure eases the pain of back labour.

LEGS OVER THE SHOULDERS
A woman of Western Samoa sits propped up with pillows, with the midwife facing her between her bent legs. If the mother grows tired, the midwife puts the mother's legs over her shoulders to help make the contractions more effective.

SITTING
Kanuri women of Borneo sit over a warmed wooden bowl; the warmth is believed to help both mother and baby.

KNEELING
Mixtecan Indian women in Mexico kneel on specially woven straw mats, with their knees wide apart and their partners sitting behind, holding them round the waist.

STANDING
On the Easter Islands, women stand with their legs apart, leaning against a male midwife.

UNDERWATER
Russian women often give birth squatting or seated in a bath, a practice that is gaining popularity throughout the West.

THE CROWNING

What can be more elating than the feeling of pushing your baby out into the world? A mother giving birth in a squatting or kneeling position can see a wisp of hair showing at the mouth of the vagina, receding, appearing again. She feels a powerful, burning sensation as the skin round the birth opening stretches to accommodate the emerging head. Many women feel torn between bearing down with all their might to get the baby out, and holding back, afraid that the head is going to rip right through them.

SOFTLY BREATHING BABY OUT

When a Jamaican baby's head becomes visible at the mouth of its mother's vagina she stops pushing, parts her lips and breathes out in a soft, even breath that helps her resist the urge to push and encourages her vaginal muscles to relax so that the baby's head can slowly, gently, ease itself out. It takes both confidence and patience simply to breathe your baby out, almost letting it make its own way into the world. But babies have been doing this for thousands of years, just as women's perinea have been stretching.

MASSAGING THE PERINEUM

Meanwhile, the Jamaican midwife massages the mother's perineum with olive oil so that it becomes supple and elastic. In seventeenth-century England the stretching perineum was massaged with oil of sweet almonds mixed with a beaten egg; in Malaysia the midwife drips coconut oil into the mother's vagina to make the passage slippery. Most midwives know how to soothe and bring much-needed blood to the tissues by holding a hot compress, or in the case of the Mansi a clod of earth is held firmly against the perineum. As the mother breathes out, scarcely pushing, her skin gradually yields to the pressure of her baby's head and stretches, little by little, until the head rotates and emerges. She might reach down and help to guide the shoulders out. The shoulders rotate, and the baby slides out into the waiting world.

The baby's head appears, stretching the vaginal opening wide.

There is blood in my eyes. A tunnel. I push into this tunnel. I bite my lips and push. There is fire and flesh ripping and no air. Out of the tunnel! All my blood is spilling out. Push! Push! It is coming! It is coming! I feel the slipperiness, the sudden deliverance, the weight is gone.
(Anais Nin)

I hold him, I hold him, until I feel he's all ready to come out, and then I go Ai! Ai! Ai! - I push hard, and plop! - it's all over.
(Algerian Jewish mother)

Ayooroorooroore eeee Ayooroorooroore!
(Wodaabe announcement of the baby's arrival, Niger)

AFTER THE BIRTH

HAIL, HAIL, HAIL, LET HAPPINESS
COME: YAO.
HAIL, LET HAPPINESS COME: YAO.
THE STRANGER WHO HAS COME, HIS
BACK IS TOWARDS THE DARKNESS:
YAO.
(Ghana prayer for the newborn)

When a woman gives birth in a squatting position, her baby is born into her immediate vision. There's no need to ask whether it's a boy or a girl - a'bow' or a 'sifter' as the Chero-kee say. The mother might greet the baby with her own hands as it slides out of her body, or she might let it drop on to warm sand, softened leaves, or a piece of bark cloth. In many cultures where a midwife attends the birth, it's she who catches the baby and lays it on the woman's belly so that mother and infant can immediately feel each other's bodies, skin to skin. The Zulu believe that it's very important for a woman to hold her child immediately, because a baby must know who its mother is.

She started to cry. I just sat there, looking at her. I thought, 'Is this my child? Who gave birth to this child?' ... I sat there and looked at her, looked and looked and looked.
(Nisa, a !Kung mother in the Kalahari Desert)

Nine months of wondering in one second solved.
(Enid Bagnold)

THE BREATH OF LIFE

As soon as a baby is born, it desperately needs to take a big fresh gulp of air into its lungs. That first breath requires five times more effort than ordinary breath. No one knows exactly why a newborn infant needs to cry as it takes its very first breath. In Osage Indian mythology, that welcome cry is believed to be the infant's prayer to Grandfather Sun or Moon Woman, a prayer it learned before coming to earth from the sky.

Some infants breathe as soon as they're pushed out of the vagina, others need some help getting the breathing process going:

The midwife slapped your footsoles, and your bald cry took its place among the elements. (Sylvia Plath)

- During the first half of this century, many doctors would hold the baby by the feet and smack it.
- The Dusin of North Borneo massage the baby's cord, hands and chest.
- Amongst the Abron of the Ivory Coast, the child is splashed with cold water.
- In Bang Chan, Thailand, the baby is shaken, but if that doesn't work, someone chews up some onions and spits them over the newborn.
- In Samoa, the midwife bounces

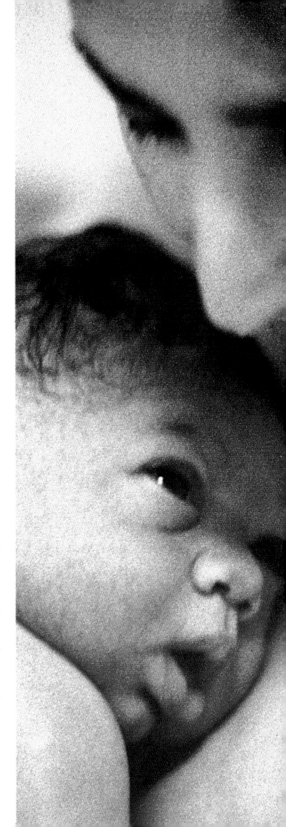

the baby four times in her hands.

- The Mixtecans of Mexico blow warm alcohol near the baby's heart.

- In Haiti, a large wooden bowl used to be inverted over the baby and beaten like a drum to wake it up.

BABY'S FRIEND - VITA! VITA!

Once the baby can breathe, its sense of smell, finely attuned to its mother's scent, helps it to find her breast quickly. In Jamaica and other places where the infant is allowed to suckle in its first moments of life, the mother's nipples are stimulated by her baby's sucking, releasing into her bloodstream oxytocin, which brings on the last few contractions to push out the afterbirth - or 'the hut of the child', as it's called in the language of one West African tribe.

THE THIRD STAGE:

The final stage of labour is potentially the most dangerous, with risks of postpartum haemorrhage. As birth attendants busy themselves with the mother and child's health and safety, mother and child meet for the very first time. The stimulation of the baby's sucking at the breast results in the production of oxytocin, which contacts the uterus, expelling the placenta, marking the end of birth. The baby's cord is cut.

Because we're so focused on getting our babies out - the product of all our labours - we often forget that birth is not over until we have delivered the placenta. Amongst the Tanala of Madagascar, who observe strict silence while a woman is giving birth, it's not until delivery of the afterbirth that everyone present starts clapping and shouting 'Vita! Vita!' - 'Finished!'

The Gabbra nomads of north-western Kenya bury a female infant's placenta under the hearth and a boy's placenta in the corral where baby camels are kept.
Both boy's and girl's future are linked to these locations.

EXPELLING THE PLACENTA

Sometimes, however, the placenta is delayed and a range of expelling techniques are employed. In the Yemen a mother is given a raw egg to swallow, to kill the worm that's been living with the baby and is making the placenta stick. Zulu, Jamaican, and many other women squat and blow into a bottle, causing the diaphragm to press in on the uterus. In other cultures an abdominal massage is given; the Hawaiian male midwife presses with his thumb on the mother's navel.

OLDER BROTHER

The placenta and the child have been living together in the womb for nine months. In the childbirth lore of many cultures they're so closely connected that the way the placenta is treated after its birth is almost as important as the way the child is treated. In Nepal, the placenta is called *bucha-co-satthi* (baby's friend) and the Malayans see the placenta as the child's older sibling. Later, if the baby smiles unexpectedly, its parents say that it's playing with its older brother, the placenta!

In the Sudan, where the afterbirth is considered to be the infant's spirit double, it should be buried in a place that represents the parents' hopes for the child. One Sudanese woman is reported to have buried her son's placenta near Khartoum University's Medical Faculty because she wanted him to be a doctor! In Hawaii it's buried under a tree, which becomes the child's tree. People in many non-literate cultures are unsure about when they were born, but know where their placentas are buried. In Yemen the placenta is left on the roof for the birds to eat, so that love will grow between the young parents.

CUTTING THE LIFELINE

The cutting of the cord that has intimately bound mother and baby during the nine months of pregnancy is in many cultures a ritual act. Who will be responsible for breaking those bonds? It may be the midwife, using a knife, a piece of bamboo, or the father's sword. The Masai midwife in Kenya chews the cord with her teeth, just as mothers themselves must have done millions of years ago. She then pronounces, 'You are now responsible for your life as I am responsible for mine', referring to the sharp contrast between the harsh environment the child is entering and the softness of the womb. Amongst the Mansi, a close friend or relative cuts the cord and becomes the child's 'navel mother'. Or it may be the new father; in a hospital birth this could be a meaningful ritual for a man in those sudden, first moments of parenthood - like cutting the ribbon that will launch his child on the voyage of life.

European folklore used to associate the length of the cut umbilical cord with the length the male child's penis could grow. (Considering that the average baby's umbilical cord is up to 35 inches long, there must have been some astonished midwives!)

Many people in different parts of the world keep not only the tool used to cut the cord but also the cord itself, either to make special healing preparations or simply as a memento. One tribe in Arizona uses the dried cord, strung with beads, to make a bracelet for the child to bite on when it starts teething. Aborigines used to make necklaces for the baby to wear to facilitate growth and avert disease. Modern medicine has also found umbilical cords valuable in saving life - their veins have become replacement arteries for victims of arteriosclerosis.

In Gabbra language, the word for placenta and midwife - aku - is the same, since both help bring you into this world.

Opposite page: Aztec stone sculpture of Tlacolteutl, goddess of childbirth.

CELEBRATIONS

Congratulations.
We knew you had
it in you.
(Dorothy Parker)

Will you celebrate the birth of your baby immediately? In many non-industrial societies, especially where infant mortality is high, it's customary to wait a few weeks before celebrating, but in other cultures parents rejoice immediately with ceremonies and celebrations that can help link the child to its family and community.

How will you celebrate the birth? Will you crack open a bottle of champagne or, as in Jamaica, a bottle of rum? Amongst the tribal people of Orissa, India, a drinking celebration is held with neighbours and friends. In Old England groaning cakes, groaning cheese and groaning beer were served to family and friends at the post-birth celebration.

In Siberia a big meal follows the birth, during which the dress worn by the mother in labour is torn down the middle to become a gown ready for breastfeeding; parents tell their children that the new baby dropped out through their mother's belly and tore her dress!

Mother and child, Oceania.

110

Mbuti pygmy mothers in Africa gather with their friends and sing special songs celebrating motherhood, but the songs of the Ibo of Nigeria are for the baby. Immediately after the newborn infant's first cry, the women at the birth start chanting and the child's kinsmen carry it to the ancestral house. A similar practice once existed in England, where the infant was immediately carried upstairs so that it would rise in life.

Immediately after birth among the Bang Chan of Thailand, the baby is laid on a winnowing tray together with the bamboo knife used to cut the cord, the clod of soil that soothed the mother's vagina as the baby's head crowned, and objects representing the parents' hopes for their child: perhaps a school book for knowledge, a needle for sharp intelligence. The winnower raises the tray into the air and circles it, saying, 'Whose child is this?', to which the mother answers, 'Mine!', catching the tray as it's dropped into her arms, and thereby claiming the infant as her own.

BIRTH ANNOUNCEMENTS

How will you announce the birth of your child? With cards? Phone calls? Blaring trumpets?

- In Ancient Rome, an olive branch hung from the front door for a boy, a strip of woollen fabric for a girl.

- The Ibo father in Nigeria takes a stem of a banana tree, ties it with a hoe and places it in front of the doorway for passers-by to see.

- The Ngoni father in Malawi stands in front of the birth hut and calls out: three times for a boy and twice for a girl.

- On the first Friday after the birth of a Malagasy child its father sends out two or three kola nuts each to male relatives and friends.

- The Dusin father in North Borneo hangs the baby's placenta in a bamboo container on the porch.

- The Tapirape father in Brazil rubs red annatto in his hair for all to see.

FACTS YOU DON'T WANT TO KNOW

CHILDBIRTH DEATHS
OVER HALF A MILLION WOMEN DIE EVERY YEAR
AS A RESULT OF PREGNANCY OR CHILDBIRTH -
99 PER CENT OF THESE DEATHS ARE IN THE
DEVELOPING WORLD, WHERE IN SOME AREAS
GIVING BIRTH IS THE LEADING CAUSE OF DEATH
AMONG WOMEN OF CHILDBEARING AGE, MAINLY
BECAUSE OF MALNUTRITION AND ANAEMIA. AN
AFRICAN WOMAN HAS A 1 IN 15 CHANCE OF
DYING DURING PREGNANCY OR CHILDBIRTH,
WHILE A NORWEGIAN WOMAN HAS A 1 IN
50,000 CHANCE.

MAMATOTO

The drama of birth is over. The cord has been cut, the first cry heard: new life has begun. An infant, wet and bloody from its long journey, experiences an overwhelming barrage of new sensations as it feels the weight of air moving across its skin, feels its lungs expand for breath, sees light, hears the sounds of the birth room. The mother - seeing, hearing, perhaps touching her baby - scarcely notices the world suddenly busying itself around her, let alone how much her body aches. She has just participated in a miracle. From the

deepest part of her comes a need to reach out and meet the tiny being skin to skin.

MAMA AND TOTO BONDING TIME

IN THE SHELTERED SIMPLICITY OF THE FIRST DAYS AFTER A BABY IS BORN, ONE SEES AGAIN THE MAGICAL SENSE OF TWO PEOPLE EXISTING ONLY FOR EACH OTHER.
(Anne Morrow Lindbergh)

Given the chance and an uninhibiting environment, we make contact with our newborn infants in a seemingly universal pattern - first exploring the baby's hands and feet with the fingertips, then with the palms of the hands stroking the whole body, then gazing into the baby's eyes, talking to it and gathering it up to the breast. This is something human

A mother's
love, a breast-
clinging child.
(Maori
proverb)

mothers do instinctively. When a parent touches a newborn infant's hypersensitive skin, the infant turns instinctively to the delicious touch and fixes its gaze on the eyes gazing into its own. And so the dance of love begins, bonding parents firmly to their babies and ensuring that the dependent newborn child will have someone to take care of its survival.

Although many women scarcely remember the events of the last few hours before birth (a forgetfulness probably caused by certain hormones coursing through the body during labour), very few can forget those first moments of motherhood. In the same way, our children's first experiences in this world probably live on, buried deep in their subconscious memories. For nine months the infant has been swimming in a warm, dark world of muffled sounds, its skin continually stimulated by the water flowing over it, its whole body rocked by its mother's movements. Perhaps we can ease its transition from this familiar and safe world into the world outside. Some primate babies actually crawl on to their mothers' abdomens as they slide out, because the soft, slack, post-birth belly feels comfortingly like being inside the womb; human babies are too undeveloped to do this by themselves. The infant needs to be held close, as it was during its last months in the uterus. In many parts of the world a massage is given immediately after birth so that the infant, feeling the gentle pressure of hands stroking and kneading its body, relaxes and its crying stops.

BONDING BY BREAST

Secure and warm against its mother's skin as it was in its uterine home, a baby in its first hour of life has a well-developed sucking reflex and a sense of smell that instinctively seeks out its mother's naked breast. This food that a woman produces from her breasts fulfils the child in every way. It has just the right balance of protein, fat and carbohydrate, adapting the ratio as the child sucks so that its needs for food and fluid are equally met. It contains agents that guard the newborn baby against diarrhoea, and transmits antibodies from the mother's system which protect it against many kinds of illness.

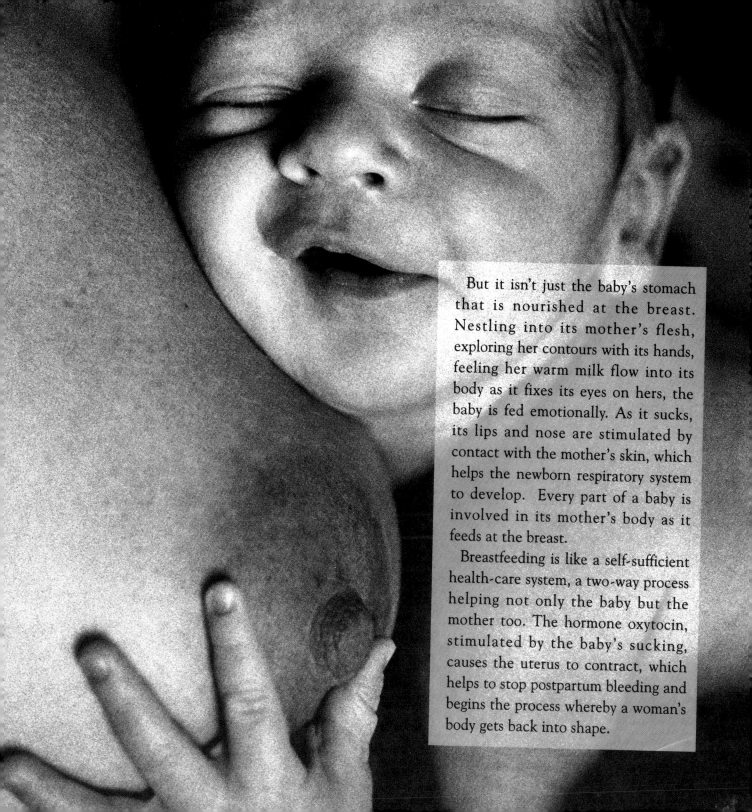

But it isn't just the baby's stomach that is nourished at the breast. Nestling into its mother's flesh, exploring her contours with its hands, feeling her warm milk flow into its body as it fixes its eyes on hers, the baby is fed emotionally. As it sucks, its lips and nose are stimulated by contact with the mother's skin, which helps the newborn respiratory system to develop. Every part of a baby is involved in its mother's body as it feeds at the breast.

Breastfeeding is like a self-sufficient health-care system, a two-way process helping not only the baby but the mother too. The hormone oxytocin, stimulated by the baby's sucking, causes the uterus to contract, which helps to stop postpartum bleeding and begins the process whereby a woman's body gets back into shape.

DON'T CUDDLE!

Bonding practices in our own society change as quickly as modern culture. In the early 1900s, attempts to cut the rate of infant mortality led doctors to isolate infants at birth so that they wouldn't be exposed to germs - even their own mothers'. By the early 1920s a new psychological theory rationalized the custom: infants needed discipline, and since mothers couldn't seem to resist cuddling them in highly damaging and sentimental ways, separation was the only answer. Once home, mothers were exhorted to quell their instincts to cuddle, kiss, or even stroke their babies - a handshake and a pat on the head were quite sufficient, wrote one doctor.

It wasn't until the 1970s that researchers realized what many indigenous cultures had never abandoned - the importance of bonding with touch for the development of the child and for the ongoing mother-child relationship.

FIRST BATH

The baby might like to be be put in a tub of water, to feel the weightlessness it felt as it floated in the womb. The Ancient Spartans ceremoniously bathed their babies in myrtle and wine - for they believed that immediately immersing an infant in a warm bath prolonged the intrauterine experience. In Haiti the infant is bathed in tepid water steeped with calabash leaves. Traditionally it was the midwife or the infant's own grandmother who bathed or massaged it, but in societies where men share in the process of birth they might use this opportunity to father their babies. Or a mother, if the setting allows, might like to share a post-birth bath with her baby, as Tanala women in Madagascar do.

The sensible way to bring up children is to treat them as young adults - never hug and kiss them. (Dr Watson, 1928)

120

BATHING BABIES

- In medieval times the infant's first bath was steeped in soothing herbs such as chamomile, lavender, or rose petals.

- The Mbuti of Zaire bathe their newborn infants immediately in the sweet-smelling water yielded by a huge vine from the forest to bond the infant to the forest from which they believe it came.

- Malaysians wash their babies in beer to protect them from disease.

- In parts of England, newborn babies' heads used to be washed in rum for good luck.

- According to Welsh folklore, a baby bathed in rainwater will grow up to be a good conversationalist!

- Ingalik melt ice for their baby's first bath, but after that they lick the baby's hands and face every morning, since melting ice consumes precious firewood.

- Chagga babies are traditionally cleaned by the mother's gentle tongue - a tradition common in Europe in the eighteenth century, when midwives were known for cleaning babies with their 'basting tongues'.

- Tapirape women in Brazil warm water in their mouths and spurt it over the infant's body.

- Ojibwa Indians in Canada bathe their babies in water infused with reindeer moss.

- The Zuni Indians of the southwestern USA would whip up yucca root in water to make suds for shampooing the infant's head, while its body was washed in fragrant juniper water.

- Cherokee babies in the United States were bathed in a decoction of golden club every new moon.

- Amongst the Dinka people of Sudan, the year following the birth of a child is called 'the bathing period'. A child who grows up weak or clumsy in build, or poorly poised, is said to have been improperly bathed as an infant.

- King Louis XI received a royal first bath - bathed in oil of roses and red wine - he was then powdered with myrrh, cumin, crushed calves' feet, and powdered snail shells.

A PERIOD OF SECLUSION

You ... are life itself when I touch you and you become heavy and warm and lean against me.
(Liv Ullman)

Both mother and baby have had a tiring journey. Both need the tranquillity and intimacy of a dimly lit environment so that they can forget about the rest of the world, relax, and delight in each other. There are years ahead in the life of the new mother and her child, and those years will be coloured by the bond that forms between them now.

Although there are crops waiting to be picked, food to be gathered, grain to be ground and fires to be built, almost every traditional society - including ours at one time - sets aside some special time for a mother and infant, and sometimes the father too. Relieved of their normal chores, they devote themselves almost exclusively to getting to know each other, recuperating from the strains of birth, and introducing the infant to the world in the gentlest possible way .

A Mbuti pygmy woman in Zaire sits in her spherical, womb-shaped leaf hut with her baby, rocking it as she rocked it while she sat rubbing her belly by the river, singing it the special song that it heard her sing while it was still inside her, letting it drink her milk and explore the feel and smell of her body. She might sit near the doorway for a while so that the baby can slowly get used to the leafy green light of its new world. But not until the third day does she leave her hut with her baby.

Different reasons are given for the practice of postnatal seclusion. The idea in many traditions is that mother and baby are still at risk from evil spirits (or what we call germs), because for a while after birth they remain tied to the spirit world and the mysterious world of woman's blood. In other words, they are still in the process of becoming. The postnatal period is seen as an extension of pregnancy; the baby is outside, but still joined to the mother's body.

Child, child, child, love I have had for my man. But now, only now, have I the fullness of love.
(Didinga, East Africa)

122

NOT OF THIS WORLD

*I remember leaving the hospital thinking, Wait. Are they going to let me just walk off with him? I don't know beans about babies! I don't have a licence to do this. We're just amateurs.
(Anne Tyler)*

New babies are not completely at home in this world. The Ibo of Nigeria say that they are still so much a part of the womb that for some time they remain in contact with unborn spirit children. Western evolutionary theory sees the newborn in a different, but similar way. Hundreds of thousands of years ago, it's believed, hominid babies lived and developed in the womb for twelve months. As the human brain and head size enlarged and woman's pelvis tipped to allow her to walk upright, it grew easier to give birth at nine months, when babies' heads could still fit through the pelvic bones.

Instead of developing inside its mother's body, the human baby has to finish its gestation outside. The newborn infant needs the security, warmth, and touch of another body in order to thrive. Indian women stay secluded with their babies in a dark, warm hut because they believe that their infants aren't ready for the bewilderingly bright lights and loud noises of the outside world.

CREATING
MAMATOTO TIME

Unfortunately, we don't all have the luxury of secluding ourselves with our babies after birth. Yahgan women in Tierra del Fuego have to get back to work gathering shellfish the day after they give birth. After time in a hospital many Western women have very little chance to cuddle with their babies because there's no one to help with household chores. Perhaps we'll evolve a way, as a society, of granting parents and babies that important time together for bonding and recovery - a way that acknowledges the father's role and his need to bond too. In Sweden, for instance, mothers and fathers are jointly given eight months' leave after the birth of their child to divide as they please.

APPRENTICESHIP
TO MOTHERHOOD

In settled agricultural societies families are large and there's always an experienced woman - relative or midwife - to stay with a new mother and baby and care for them. In the Sudan, a woman's only responsibility is to feed her baby while her mother or sister cares for her and receives visitors bringing daily gifts of goat's or camel's milk to build up her strength. The Mixtecan midwife helps the new mother take a series of ritual sweatbaths, and shows her how to care for her child. In this way the period after birth serves not only as an opportunity for mother and child to grow close and rest, but also as an apprenticeship for motherhood.

Right: In medeival times, mothers lay in bed for the first week after giving birth and received help from midwives and neighbours.
Left: Chhetri mothers of Humla, Nepal, share a laugh while helping each other care for babies.

I myself know of no greater misery than nursing a child, the physical collapse ... is often at the bottom of the drinking habits of which we hear so much. (Mrs. Patton, 1913)

MOTHERCARE

Western medicine tends to place more emphasis on the care of the pregnant woman than on the health of a woman who's just given birth, and those first weeks after birth can be debilitating if the body is not given an opportunity to recover. Almost every system in the body is readapting to non-pregnancy. Besides the strain on muscles and tissues from the birth itself, many changes are taking place in a woman's body during the post-partum period. The uterus has to contract back to its original size, nutrients are being channelled into milk, hormones are finding a new balance, and hair and skin begin to change, as they did in pregnancy. When a new mother neglects her body's special needs during this time she can suffer in all sorts of ways, both physical and psychological.

SINGING THE BLUES

The Malaysians see postpartum depression or 'baby blues', for instance, as a spiritual affliction caused by physical weakness. According to the Malaysian system of medicine, when the body is weak the spirit is poorly guarded. Anything that causes the new mother sadness or anger makes her even more vulnerable. If her spirit succumbs, she loses her appetite, cries a lot, and without knowing why she finds it impossible to look after her infant. Malaysian women who suffer from postpartum blues are helped with incantations and magically treated water. If this doesn't work, a spirit-raising seance is held. The mother, in a trance state, is encouraged to express all her most negative emotions - her angers, her fears and anxieties, her ambivalent feelings about being a mother.

126

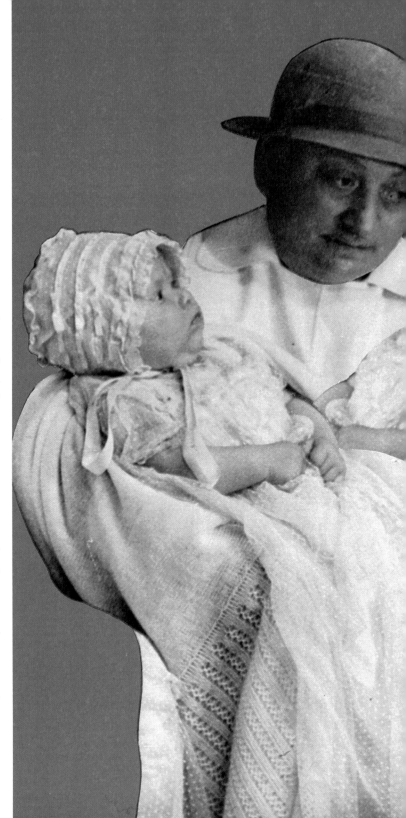

Fifty to 75 per cent of new mothers get the baby blues, one in ten develops postnatal depression, two in every thousand develops severe psychosis. Postnatal illness can vary in severity from 'baby blues', which usually occurs around the third or fourth day after the baby is born and lasts for about two weeks, to a depression lasting several months. Postnatal depression may be characterized by feelings of remoteness, panic attacks, insomnia, a chronic desire for sleep, violent feelings about the baby or lack of any bond with it. Therapy and medical attention can help.

BODYCARE

How can we care for ourselves during this vulnerable period? What will help you feel good about your body so that you feel good about yourself as a woman?

It isn't easy for many Western women to let themselves be mothered, or to devote time to looking after themselves when there's a new baby to be cared for. But just as our feelings about our pregnant bodies affect our pregnancies, our feelings about our bodies as mothers will affect our changed relationships with our lovers, our children, ourselves and the world to which we hope to return.

This is recognized in many traditional cultures, where fragrant baths and hairwashes, strengthening herbs, special foods, and massages with healing oils or pastes help the new mother to feel comfortable in her own body. Both the specific aches of the postpartum period and our general sense of physical well-being need attention. In Java, the new mother's body is massaged all over with riceflour paste and a root that makes the skin tingle. A mudpack with added roots and herbs is applied to her forehead, and she's given a glass of wine daily and a potion of ginger, garlic, roses, sugar, and pepper to make her feel good.

MOTHER HEALING

Like women in the West, most tribal women don't have the opportunity to take weeks off with their babies. They need to be up and about quickly, but first they have to help their bodies recover. How will you speed up the process of recovery so that you can get back to work quickly without paying the price later?

127

- Will you give yourself abdominal massages to help your uterus shrink and ask someone, perhaps your partner, to pamper your muscles with all-over body massages?

- Will you use an abdominal binder to support your belly, or do exercises to strengthen abdominal muscles?

- Will you use heat treatments to soothe your contracting uterus?

- Will you seek out herbal teas to tone uterine muscle and strengthen your internal systems?

- Will you feed your body with healthful, nourishing foods?

MASSAGE

The aches and pains we feel after birth will go, but we can help them to pass more quickly. In fact, it's not surprising that the body needs quite a bit of attention after all the muscle and skin-stretching of pregnancy. In Malaysia, a specially trained masseur comes every day to knead the mother's abdomen. In Europe and North America, friction and kneading were popular until early this century. To ease aching joints, Jicarillo Indian women in Mexico have their bodies massaged with a rubbing lotion made from the leaves and seeds of boiled angelpod.

Midwives in the Maikal Hills, India, and in parts of the American South-west, press their oil-covered heads and knees into the woman's abdomen to shrink the uterus. If there's nobody to help us we could knead our own abdomens, as Tahitian women do while they bathe in the river; massaging the abdomen with oils also helps to heal the scars of stretched belly skin. Massage can help the new mother to relax and feel good about her body. Some women massage their partners, too. During those first, sometimes strained weeks of parenthood, it's a wonderful way of exchanging loving feelings.

BINDING THE BELLY

After each of her *twenty* postnatal massages, a Mayan women has her abdomen tied with a supportive sash, just as she did during her pregnancy. Women from Africa to Japan - and until early in this century English women too - say the sash feels comforting and relaxing, and eases abdominal cramps.

ROASTING CRAMPS AWAY

It's not unusual to suffer from mild cramps as the uterus contracts. Gentle heat as well as massage can ease those cramps; traditionally, heating stones, hot leaves, or bags of warm sand were laid on the belly. In fact, warmth in general is seen as beneficial in many cultures where it's believed that a woman is internally 'cold' after birth. A Mexican Seri Indian mother suffering from an aching back places heated stones on her belly and lies on top of leafy creosote-bush branches placed over a small pit filled with warm ashes. In Indonesia a new mother is traditionally 'roasted': she lies for part of each day on a bed over a smoking fire. This is supposed to dry up the uterine discharge, improve the circulation, shrink the uterus, and tighten the woman's vagina so that lovemaking will be as pleasurable as it was before.

WOMB CARE

- In sixteenth-century England, women were given strained hog's dung with sugar and nutmeg to prevent postpartum haemorrhage.

- New mothers in Bang Chan, Thailand, drink a filtrate of tamarind, salt, and water to strengthen the womb.

- Some women in New Mexico drink sweet basil tea to ease uterine cramps.

- Seri Indians of Mexico drink tea made from seep willow to stop blood after childbirth.

- Oil of Roses is a traditional European tonic for ovaries and uterus.

- To help expel uterine blood, Jicarillo Indian women chew the roots of wild geranium.

- Zuni women drink hot juniper tea continuously to make the blood flow after birth.

- Arab women in Saudi Arabia traditionally insert rock salt in the shape of an egg into the vagina after meals for ten to forty days after birth to prevent infection. The salt purifies the womb of 'rotten blood', the women say.

Your womb will shrink back to half its pregnant size before the newborn infant is a week old. By the time the baby is a month old, the uterus may be as small as it was the day the embryo first moved in.

129

HEALING
'THE PRIVIE PLACE'

Women who have perineal tears or stitches from episiotomies might be surprised by how much they hurt for the first few days, making it hard to imagine ever making love again. We can help ourselves to heal faster by bathing our perinea and applying heat treatments - Jamaican women, for instance, squat over buckets of steaming-hot water. Haitian women put leaves of the castor oil plant in their baths - these are known also as *palma Christi* leaves or Christ's Hand, because of their association with the great healer. In Bang Chan, women put 'tapping fruits' between their legs every day for a few days to cure the birth wound - balls of tamarind leaves, phlai and salt wrapped in cloth.

ICONS OF ABUNDANCE

Throughout history, women have prayed for an abundance of milk with which to nourish their babies. Japanese women buy special breast icons to offer at the temple, and Jordanian women wear white pebbles from the Grotto of Milk in Bethlehem as amulets, since legend has it that some drops of Mary's milk spilled there. Artemis, goddess of the crescent moon and of plenty, was worshipped as a mother deity in her temple in Izmir, Turkey, where a statue shows her entire torso graced with dozens of fruit-like breasts. The famous stone figurines known as Venuses of Willendorf, with their breast-like heads, may have been Neanderthal woman's lactation amulets.

RELEASING THE FLOW

The Jicarillo of Mexico believe that a grandmother or another old woman relative can suckle the mother 'to clean out the breasts' if her milk isn't flowing well, stimulating the glands that produce milk. Some women just let the baby suck the dry nipple until the milk establishes itself; in one New Guinea tribe, even women who have adopted infants find that by continually giving them their breasts to suckle they can stimulate a good supply of milk within a few weeks.

In some cultures, including Nigeria, women have their breasts vigorously massaged by female relatives during the weeks before and after birth. Bathing the breasts by sponging them, as Azande women do, or relaxing in a warm tub, can get the milk flowing. If this doesn't help, the woman is given a wet nurse, someone who will nurse her child - if possible, a woman related to the mother.

LIKE WET NURSE, LIKE BABY

Because a woman imparts something of herself to the baby when she feeds it with her own milk, wet nurses are seen as having a special relationship to the infant, a kind of blood-link. Amongst the Mixtecan Indians, the Sudanese, and in many other cultures it's believed that the child inherits physical characteristics from the woman who feeds it. In nineteenth-century Europe, red-headed wet nurses were avoided for this reason, for it was believed that they had flaring-hot tempers which would be passed on to the suckling child. In fact the drunkenness of Caligula, the notorious debauched ruler of Ancient Rome, was rumoured to have been drawn from his wet nurse's breast.

WE ARE WHAT WE EAT

Of course, if we are what we eat, then our children do get something of us in our milk. Many of the things we ingest, including medicines and harmful chemicals, find their way into breastmilk, and most cultures have as many, if not more, food taboos for the lactating (milk-producing) period as they do for pregnancy. On the other hand, we can give our babies good things through our milk too. Arab herders, who encourage their flocks to pasture on rosemary because it makes the milk taste good, also recommend plenty of rosemary in a breastfeeding woman's diet for its tonic effects on the child.

BREAST CARE
- Magar women of Nepal rub apricot oil on their nipples to relieve cracking.
- Ibo women of Nigeria rub chewed palm kernal fibre over their nipples.
- Jicarillo women of Mexico rub ashes of burned red top grass to ease soreness.

MAMAPAPA

She told me to go take some drugs and chant to my forest spirits. She is still stingy with her vagina. (Yanomamo Indian man, shunned by his wife during the post-natal sex taboo)

How soon will you make love again? Every culture has its own answer to this question - anywhere from six weeks, according to Western medicine, by which time the risk of uterine infection has passed, to the three-year postnatal taboo in American Sioux society, the time when a baby is weaned. If the mother were to get pregnant again before this, the child in the womb would deprive the child at the breast of the milk on which it depends.

For new mothers, these taboos can be quite welcome at times. Many breastfeeding women, for instance, feel less ready to share with their husbands the body that's being shared with the baby, especially for a few weeks after birth when the perineum is still tender and the body in flux. Men too might feel inhibited - 'afraid of the blood that's healing', as Nisa, a !Kung bush-woman, said.

But this doesn't have to mean that women and men can't be close after the birth of their child. Arapesh men in New Guinea sleep and cuddle with their wives and babies throughout the one-year period of abstinence. A man might massage his wife's recovering body, helping them to come together through gentle touch.

PAPATOTO: BECOMING A FATHER

What do new fathers do while new mothers are cooing to their babies? What is the man's role during this intensely maternal period after birth? Some men leave the business of babycare to the women. Their role is ritual; the Muslim father, for instance, places a piece of date in his infant's mouth to show him how sweet life can be. His main role is to provide good things for his wife to eat so that her milk will be rich.

The giving of food is an important symbolic act demonstrating deep care - for without food there can't be life. A few days after the birth of the Kaluli child in Borneo, its parents take it on an expedition to a forest camp where they find crayfish and sago grubs for the father to feed to the baby over the next few days - an opportunity for him to form a nurturing relationship with his infant.

Modern Western fathers also like to give food to their babies, holding them in their arms at night while their wives rest, and feeding them from bottles filled with formula or expressed mother's milk, stored for the purpose. In this way, the father is

co-operating in his wife's return to strength. Mbuti pygmy men in Zaire help to strengthen their wives and babies by sprinkling special juices over them from vines cut in the forest. Amongst the Indians of Brazil, the link between father and child is so strong that the word for child means 'little father'.

A father in our culture can be initiated into parenthood through his involvement in the birth process. But for a few days following the birth, while mother and baby are in the hospital, he can feel a little at a loss. Suddenly he is a father - what does that mean, and what's he supposed to do? The Ainu man in Japan retires after the birth to a friend's hut, where he spends twelve days in seclusion, meditating on fatherhood. Just as the mother gave the baby its body during pregnancy, now he gives his soul to the child.

JOINING THE COMMUNITY OF FATHERS

The Arapesh father of New Guinea chooses a man who has children to be his own ritual 'father'. The old father bathes the new father in aromatic herbs, purifying him and anointing him with white paint. After the new father has caught an eel, symbolic of the phallus, he formally becomes one of the community of fathers.

BABY BODYCARE

IF THIS CHILD THRIVES UNDER YOUR DEVOTED CARE, MAY ITS FACE SHINE. MAY IT UPROOT THE NIGHTSHADE BUSHES WITH ITS BRUSHING THIGH. MAY IT NOT BECOME ILL. (West African prayer to Chagga deities, to protect the newborn)

LEARNING FROM SISTERS

In our culture, inexperienced mothers can feel a little confused about how to look after babies. A link is missing in the chain by which the tried and tested cultural lore of childcare is passed down. Modern

mothers make up for it by exchanging tips with friends, and even with strangers in baby magazine columns. But what can we learn from our own past, and from women in other cultures, to boost our own confidence?

CARING FOR THE STUMP

We bring the baby home with a cord stump that has to be kept dry and protected from infection until, after a few days or a couple of weeks, it withers and falls. Western doctors usually recommend alcohol to clean the area around the stump, but to some women this can seem like harsh treatment for a tiny baby. The Bedouins sprinkle dried powdered rosemary on and around the cord; it acts both as an astringent, drying it so that it falls sooner, and as an antiseptic. During the seventeenth century a powder of Bole Armeniacke, Sanguis Draconis and myrrh was used.

A Mien mother cares for her child. Left: A Surma man of Ethiopia has his body painted with chalk and water.

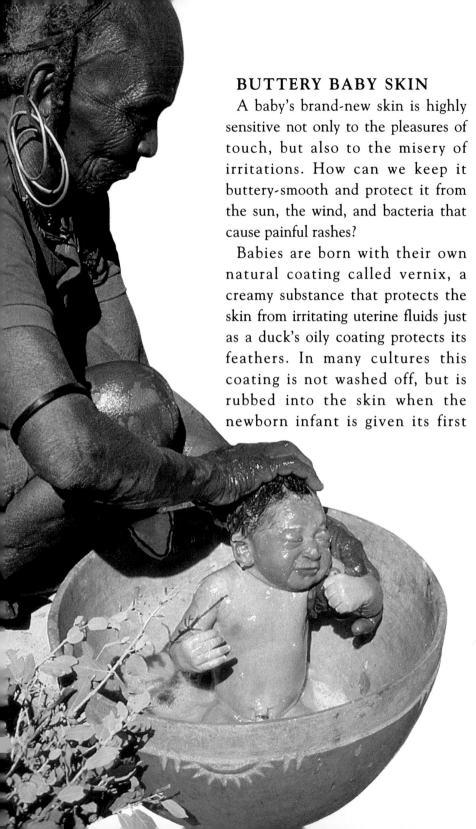

BUTTERY BABY SKIN

A baby's brand-new skin is highly sensitive not only to the pleasures of touch, but also to the misery of irritations. How can we keep it buttery-smooth and protect it from the sun, the wind, and bacteria that cause painful rashes?

Babies are born with their own natural coating called vernix, a creamy substance that protects the skin from irritating uterine fluids just as a duck's oily coating protects its feathers. In many cultures this coating is not washed off, but is rubbed into the skin when the newborn infant is given its first massage. In cultures where the vernix is washed off - or licked off, as it is in Chagga society - the covering is replaced with special herbal pastes, butter, or natural oils. In Siberia babies are rubbed with fermented tamarind after the vernix is removed. During the Middle Ages newborn babies were washed and then rubbed all over with oil of myrtle and roses, or a mixture of salt and honey; during the fifteenth century one of the midwife's important tasks was to 'anoint' the infant's body with oil of almond after licking it clean with her 'basting tongue'.

Hawaiians smear kukui oil into their babies' bodies, and spread arrowroot in all the creases so that the tender skin doesn't chafe. Some people believe that by dusting the baby's skin you can make sure the smooth body doesn't get too hairy. For this reason the American Hopi father used to bring powdery grey mountain ashes from a nearby extinct volcano called Baby Ashes Mountain, and for three days this powder was rubbed into the infant's skin, apparently making it very soft and clean through a process of exfoliation.

A Wodaabe newborn from Niger is born with undeveloped pigment in its skin.

PROTECTION IN THE DAYS OF NEED

Some people believe that by paying attention to a baby's body you can protect it from evil spirits, or from simply vanishing from the world. Bedouin Arabs smear their babies with a mixture of oil and salt during the seven 'days of need, danger and death' following its birth. Perhaps one of the most important things we can learn from looking at the variety of ways people care for their babies' bodies is that as long as we do care for them in a way they seem to like, it doesn't matter too much what we do.

LANGUAGE OF TOUCH

When a woman spends time caring for her baby's body - bathing and rubbing it, massaging its limbs as the Maori of New Zealand do so that they'll grow lithe and supple, wrapping it in soft leaves or cloths and unwrapping it again for another massage - she is communicating with it through the only language it knows: the language of the senses. Through touch, Australian Aborigines impart important social values to their infants. Placing her hand gently on the child's forehead, a mother or grandmother speaks softly to the infant: 'You must give, you must share everything'; on the mouth: 'Don't use bad language'; on the eyes: 'Don't concentrate your gaze on the things of others.'

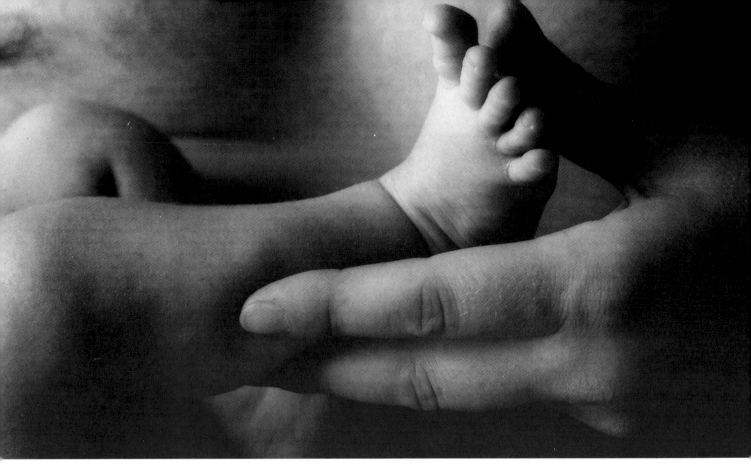

INFANT MASSAGE

Massage is a crucial and routine part of infant care from Africa to India and Indonesia, from Central and South America to Australia and the Soviet Union - in fact, there are few places in the world where babies are not routinely massaged during the first few months and years of life. If one were to ask women in these different cultures why they massage their babies there would be several different answers, some to do with health and protection from the elements, others with emotional well-being, and still others with beauty - the people of India and Hawaii, for example, believe that a baby's face can be made more beautiful through massage, and so from the moment of birth the head, nose, mouth and eyes are squeezed into shape. Maori infant massage used to focus on knees and ankles, since it was thought that rubbing them gently morning and

If you massage the baby, it will make his bones strong. We try to massage the baby twice a day until he is two years old. We massage the baby with mustard oil and breast milk. (Newar woman of Nepal)

evening for a few years would keep the joints supple and the child graceful. In Bali, massage is traditionally given to a baby troubled by tummy pains. Yurok Indian babies had their legs massaged every day from the twentieth day on so that they would learn to crawl early, and mothers in the Soviet Union are taught by doctors to massage their babies during their first days of life in order to help develop the central nervous system.

Often massage happens moments after birth. Immediately after the birth of a Bornu baby in Nigeria, for instance, the mother's helpers warm their hands over a dish of hot coals and gently proceed to press the child's body. Babies new to this world need, enjoy, and yearn to be stroked, to feel the soothing touch of skin brushing their skin, just as in their uterine homes they felt the water moving over their bodies. And parents need it, too - massaging the new baby lets a mother or father grow close and comfortable with this tiny, fragile body, communicating to it in the language it knows best.

Dzoomkyet, a Nyniba mother married to five brothers, cradles her newborn. Humla, Nepal.

139

CRYING AND COMFORTING

Although most people agree that crying is a normal human response to sadness, pain, or fear, different cultures have their own interpretations for the crying of infants. The Mansi people in Siberia, for instance, believe that a baby begins to cry at night because the soul of a dead person entering its body has disturbed it; this happens to all babies. Some English people used to believe that children cried to exercise their lungs, while the common Western explanation from the early days of this century until the 1970s was that a child cries simply to get its parents' attention, and that if it is picked up it will only learn to cry more. Now we believe that, as the Yanomamo Indians of Brazil say, a child is born with a will that is completely innocent and ignorant. Children cry because crying is their language of need, a survival language. When we answer that need, a child quickly grows to understand that it is safe in the world.

A loud noise on one end and no sense of responsibility at the other.
(Ronald Knox)

*Darling, why
are you crying?
Darling, is it
for bathing you
are crying?
Child, what are
you crying for?
Child, is it for
sleep?
Darling,
Ro-ro-ro.
(Veddas lullaby,
Sri Lanka)*

SIXTH SENSE

Of course, the way we interpret our babies' cries influences our response. The Mansi perform a ritual to find out whose soul has entered the baby. Once they've discovered the answer, the child's crying is said to stop. When we in the West saw crying as a baby's way of getting spoiled we chose to ignore it. Just as mothers who listen to their babies quickly learn to distinguish different cries for different kinds of needs, mothers who maintain a close physical contact with their infants, carrying them against their bodies or holding them in their arms, soon develop a sensitivity to the baby's slightest restlessness. A bushwoman can sense a change in her infant's breathing pattern, and she can feel its body tense before it even opens its mouth to cry.

THE DANGERS OF CRYING

Jamaican women believe that if you leave a child to cry the duppies, or ghosts, might hear it and come to take it away. Similarly, the Yanomamo Indians say that when a child cries its soul can easily escape, and when that happens the child can die, leaving its soul to wander endlessly in the jungle. Therefore the baby must be soothed, its crying stopped immediately. It's quite possible that in our own past - and still amongst some hunter-gatherer populations - an infant's cries may have brought the danger of predators. 'Do not cry, my child! What are you crying for? If you wail, the leopard will devour your mother', goes a Chagga lullaby.

*I love children.
Especially
when they cry -
for then
someone takes
them away.
(Nancy
Mitford)*

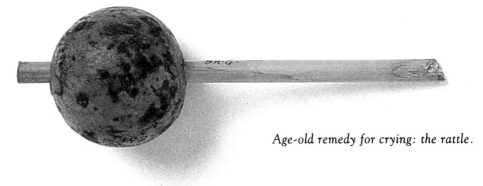

Age-old remedy for crying: the rattle.

141

COMFORTING BUILDS TRUST

We have no fear of predators in our world, but the infant's need for comfort still exists. Anthropologists, looking at cultures where a baby's comfort needs are quickly and tenderly indulged - even before it cries - have found that by the third month of life these babies cry less than Western infants. Instead of learning that only when they demand will someone respond, they come to trust that they will be cared for. How can we soothe our babies so that they'll cry less?

Boran mother and child of Kenya.

ROCK-A-BYE BABY

The baby in the womb experienced no stillness, because even when its mother was resting there was the movement of the uterine waters all around it. When we rock babies in our arms we tend to do it at a speed which is the same as the rhythm of a mother's walk as she carries the child in her womb. The mechanical swings of Western babycare are also designed to duplicate that rhythm.

The kinaesthetic stimulation that a baby gets when it's rocked, jounced or jiggled can be soothing or arousing, depending on the state of the baby at the time. This means that whether the baby is bored or tense, movement will help it. Perhaps this is one reason why infants cry less in parts of the world where they are continuously attached to the mother's body. The Zinacantan baby of South America, for instance, is rocked rhythmically on its mother's back as she walks or grinds corn.

THE SOOTHING RHYTHM OF THE HEART

Parents seem to know intuitively what their babies need. When you pick up your crying infant it's almost automatic to hold it to the left side of your chest, where it can hear the soothing rhythm of your heart. Madonna and child images show the same tendency. There was always a background of gentle sound to lull the baby in the womb - sounds coming from the outside, and the rhythm of the mother's heartbeat. That's why singing, humming, murmuring and cooing to our babies calms them.

NAPPIES

Love twisted suddenly inside her, compelling her to reach into the crib and lift up the moist, breathing weight ... the smells of baby powder and clean skin and warm flannel mingled with the sharp scent of wet nappy. (Rosie Thomas)

Often babies cry simply because they are wet and need their nappies changed. Iroquois Indians used to line their cradles with moss, a natural disinfectant, which acted as a nappy. In the sixteenth century nappies were called tailclouts because they were often made from husbands' old shirts. In the 1920s most nappies were made of Turkish towelling. Today, four out of five UK babies wear disposable nappies, and in the USA, 18 billion disposable nappies are sold each year. Thirty million trees are used each year in the manufacture of disposable nappies, which cause even greater environmental damage in landfill sites where they do not decompose. Perhaps it's time to learn the trick of Ugandan mothers who carry their babies around with them so close that they claim to sense when their child needs to urinate or defecate - at which time they simply take them off their back. It would certainly keep down the cost of nappies ...

The baby wakes up in the wee wee hours of the morning. (Robert Robbins)

SLEEP

Tiny babies don't go to sleep at convenient times, like when their parents want to or when adults are too busy to tend to them. They nod in and out of sleep, day and night, waking from hunger or just because something happening inside their own bodies has disturbed them.

Although this kind of pattern - or lack of it - can make life exhausting for a parent, it's a pattern that's well adapted to the kind of society in which infants are carried around much of the day, and sleep in their mother's arms at night.

A !Kung infant, for instance, is nearly always in an upright position during the day. But being cradled on its mother's lap, or propped up in a sling at her side while she goes about her daily work, doesn't stop a baby from dozing off whenever it needs to. In fact, the movements of the mother's body soothe the infant, so sleep comes more easily. By night, sleeping face to face with its mother on a skin on the ground, it scarcely needs to wake her with its cries before she sleepily gives it her breast.

Sleep sweet in my arms, which are surrounding you like soft silk.
(Greek lullaby)

People who say they sleep like a baby usually don't have one.
(Leo Burke)

Where does your baby sleep?

- Brazilian babies sleep cradled in hammocks with their mothers.
- Japanese infants share their parents' futons.
- North American Indian babies slept strapped into wicker cradleboards padded with cedar bark and embellished with turquoise.
- The Seri Indian infant in Mexico sleeps in a shallow basket filled with clean sand and lined with cloth.
- Santhali babies in Bihar, India, sleep on a bed made from bamboo struts and woven with jute.

- Before 1800 in England, babies of noble heritage slept in gilded cradles under fur coverlets.
- Babies in New Zealand sleep on sheepskins, which help them to retain their body heat and gain weight faster.
- Mansi babies in Siberia spend their first weeks sleeping in a tiny birch-bark cradle, under a swan-skin coverlet. At the end of that period the cradle is hidden in the woods, together with the cradles of all the other babies who have been born in the village.

Although small babies are incapable of trying to stay awake, sometimes they find it hard to go to sleep, especially if they're overtired or wound up from a lot of excitement or attention. How can we help our babies fall asleep?

FROM
SOOTHING SYRUPS
TO WASHING MACHINES

In Colonial America mothers gave fretful babies special 'soothing syrups' containing opium, morphine, chloroform and cannabis. Opium was given to Italian infants in the sixteenth and seventeenth centuries, and is still occasionally given to babies by busy mothers in parts of India.

A custom in Western industrialized society has been to put the infant in its cot and let it cry itself to sleep. Our society values independence and self-sufficiency, and expects children to learn very early in life that they can comfort themselves. In tribal cultures, which depend on individuals coming together and helping each other, it's natural for parents to welcome their children's need to be comforted. Mothers in Fiji massage their babies before sleep so that they'll settle down and rest well through the night. Cradles and hammocks, or baskets suspended on ropes from the ceiling, are gently rocked, relaxing the baby. One American mother found that putting her baby to sleep on top of a tumbling washing machine had the same effect.

Lucky me!

LULLABIES

I WOULD PUT MY OWN CHILD TO
SLEEP,
AND NOT THE SAME AS THE WIVES
OF CLOWNS DO,
UNDER A YELLOW BLANKET AND
SHEET OF TOW,
BUT IN A CRADLE OF GOLD ROCKED
BY THE MIND.
(Irish lullaby)

All over the world, people take their children into their laps or arms and sing them lullabies - lullabies they heard as a child, or any repetition of words or sounds to make a rhythm like the rocking of a cradle. Korean mothers repeat the word 'sleep', 'sleep', over and over again, perhaps patting the baby lightly on the stomach at the same time. 'We tell them stories and rock them,' said Sumi, a Santhali mother in India. 'There are stories about the land and the forest, and we make up stories about the gods who roam in our lands.' At night in a Sudanese Dinka village, a song can nearly always be heard drifting out of a dark hut into the silence, long after the baby has fallen asleep.

DREAM FACES

What's happening in a baby's inner world as it sleeps? Parents often wonder about this because of all the faces a baby makes while it's dozing. Some people believe these are caused by dreams; the gypsies traditionally put sprigs of rosemary under infants' pillows to ensure that their dreams will be pleasant. According to Welsh folklore, when a baby laughs or frowns in its sleep it means that the fairies are kissing it. The Tibetans say that a dwarfish creature called a rep-thang (small fairytale creature) irritates the baby, making it frown. But when the rep-thang plays, the baby smiles.

Pakistani infant deep in slumber.

RETURN TO THE WORLD

At some point every woman has to leave her place of seclusion and get back to work. Gardens need tending, children have to be cared for, grain must be ground, and jobs returned to; women play central roles in most non-industrial economies, as they do in our own today. Some women start to miss the busy life of the marketplace or the office. How do you know when it's time to go back to the world?

Since the whole community - and especially the family - has a stake in the well-being of mother and infant, it may not be up to the mother to decide when she and her baby can leave their place of seclusion. In the Muslim world the period of seclusion traditionally lasts forty days, by which time a woman's 'impure' uterine discharge has usually stopped flowing. Although the 'lying-in' period in Great Britain is traditionally three days (even in the sixteenth century) a woman might see her six-week check-up at forty-two days as a signal that she's ready to get back to normal life.

Or she might take her cue from the baby. In some cultures mother and infant can join the world when the baby's cord has dried and dropped off, usually between five and ten days following birth, or when the fontanelle has hardened; many believe that evil spirits can enter the child through the soft spot on the head. In the Gold Coast, parents feel by the end of seven days that the infant has decided to stay on this earth, and mother and baby rejoin the community.

Three months after the birth of her child, the Chagga woman's head is shaved and crowned with a bead tiara, she is robed in an ancient skin garment worked with beads, a staff such as the elders carry is put in her hand, and she emerges from her hut for her first public appearance with her baby. Proceeding slowly towards the market, they are greeted with songs such as are sung to warriors returning from battle. She and her baby have survived the weeks of danger. The child is no longer a vulnerable, jumpy newborn - a 'red-faced' as the Dusin of Borneo say - but a baby who has learned what love means, has smiled its first smiles, and is now ready to learn about the bright, loud world outside.

Facts You don't Want to Know

Bottle-Feeding is Killing Babies in the Third World

UNICEF estimates that one million babies die each year as a result of bottle-feeding with infant formula. Increasing numbers of women in the Third World are giving up breastfeeding, seduced by the pictures of fat babies on the side of baby-milk cans. Bottle-feeding is seen as more modern and liberating by women who are moving into the consumer culture of the cities. The trend is having a devastating effect on the health of infants due to unsterilized feeding equipment, water from contaminated supplies, and overdilution of milk powder. A bottle-fed baby is twenty-five times more likely to die than a breastfed one in poor countries.

A
New
Stranger
Has
Arrived

After weeks of intense emotional and physical closeness, women return to the world with their infants, and to the routine of work and community life. Many cultures recognize this point as yet another transition around which ceremonies and celebrations take place. In Malaysia the mother's 'roasting bed' is dismantled and a forked stick is rubbed amongst the ashes and tossed through the window, taking the dangers of the postnatal period out of the house. In Guatemala, all the jars, the knife, the bowls and heating

stones used at birth are taken outside and dedicated to a spring or river. The child, born into the close world of its mother's arms days or weeks ago, is about to be reborn into a far wider world. To signify this rebirth - and perhaps also to help the new mother come to terms with her experience of the birth itself - the Malaysian woman and her infant pass through a circle of string, symbolic of the cervix.

LEAVING THE WORLD OF SPIRITS: RITUALS OF INTRODUCTION

The baby has formed its bonds with the mother; now it's time to get to know the people amongst whom it will live and grow. Often the child is first presented to the gods who will protect it as it leaves the world of spirits. For generations people in many parts of the world have used magically treated water to purify the new baby. Christians purify babies for God through the rite of baptism - a rite far older than Christianity. European baptism lore still holds hints of its ancient pagan past with superstitions like: it's lucky to baptize a baby at the full moon, or a baby washed in baptismal water will have a good complexion.

BATHING THE SKIN OF THIS CHILD OF THE GODS,
BATHING IT IN THE LIVING WATERS OF TANE-
LISTEN TO THE WINDS THE GODS HAVE SENT,
THE SOFT WIND FROM THE EAST,
WHICH IS BLOWN THIS WAY
TO GIVE FEELING TO THE SKIN OF THE CHILD.
(Tahitian baptismal chant)

BONDING WITH THE ELEMENTS

In some cultures anointing with water is a way of dedicating the child to the earth itself. The Jicarillo Indians of Mexico, for instance, would pour water from a sacred female river and a sacred male river over the infant's head. Throughout the ceremony songs were sung about the long-lived sacred rivers and about the earth's riches, pollen and iron ore, which were ceremonially sprinkled on the faces of mother, father, and baby.

We in the West have mostly given up our ancient rituals of intro-duction; might this explain why women in our culture often experience the return to society as an anticlimax? With no ceremonies to mark the occasion, there's no way of expressing the transformations that have taken place. On the surface, the world hasn't changed; and yet to the mother, everything feels different.

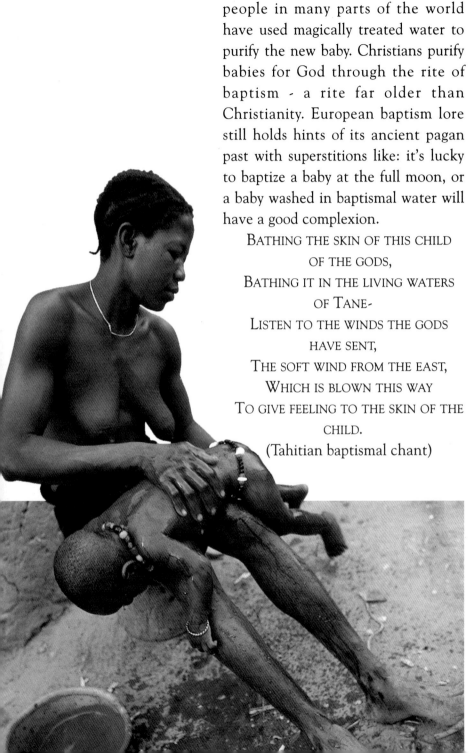

A Dogon mother of Mali bathes her young infant.

NEW PERSON

In many cultures the mother must be reintroduced into the community, for she has become a new person. To mark the occasion, she might take a special bath and shave her head, as Qemant women in Ethiopia do. The Nuba mothers of Sudan decorate their bodies with special incision marks which proudly display their new status. The Aborigine mother and child paint themselves with sacred white clay before returning to the clan. For her child's introduction will also mark her reunion with her husband, the new father.

CELEBRATION

A big party is thrown for the introduction of a Sudanese baby and its new mother. Family and friends celebrate late into the night, feasting on a sacrificial sheep and dancing to the sound of a live band - amplified if possible so that the whole street can join in.

Amongst the Ibo of Nigeria, a party is held for all the babies and toddlers under three years of age, for they are believed to be psychically linked to the newborn. Or, as amongst the Mbuti pygmies of Zaire, the child might simply be passed around a small circle of people close to the parents, so that they too can hold it in their arms, kiss it, and let it experience the comfort that other bodies besides its own mother's can provide.

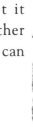

BIRTH TREES

At the edge of each Ibo village in Nigeria is a grove of banana trees, each one named after the child for whom it was planted. The grove belongs communally to the small children of the village, and is their special play area.

From Switzerland and Sweden to Java and Africa, trees are planted as a way of commemorating the introduction of the child into society. In Switzerland an apple tree is planted for a girl, a nut tree for a boy. As the child grows, so does the tree. Indonesian people believe that the destinies of children and their birth trees are intertwined. In some cultures the person's age is estimated by the rings in the trunk of their birth tree.

AND WHEN THEY NAME YOU GREAT
WARRIOR,
THEN WILL MY EYES BE WET WITH
REMEMBERING.
AND HOW SHALL WE NAME YOU,
LITTLE WARRIOR?
SEE, LET US PLAY AT NAMING.
(Didinga, East Africa)

156

NAMING THE CHILD

Is a child different after he or she has been given a name? In the language of the Kafirs of Afghanistan, the word for 'to name' means literally 'to pour into'. A name is connected to a child's soul and gives him or her an identity; many people consider the nameless child to be like a floating spirit, unrooted and unprotected. The English, for example, once believed that butterflies were the souls of babies who had died before christening.

In fact, historians surmise that it was in order to protect babies that we developed the custom of naming them as soon after birth as possible. Once upon a time that was easy because there weren't a lot of names to choose from, and many babies were simply named after a close relative. The hunter-gatherer !Kung people, who have only thirty-five names for each sex from which to choose, also name their newborn infants after a grandfather, aunt or other close relative. They believe that sharing a name with someone creates a special kind of bond. For the same reason, the Thonga of South Africa like to let a friend of the family give their own name to the child at the time of birth, creating a close relationship between the two that's cemented once a year with the giving of a present.

BELLY STICKING OUT

Dusin babies in North Borneo, on the other hand, aren't formally named until they're five, when it's believed that a child's character begins to form. Until then they're called by a nickname based on some funny habit: 'holding on tightly', or 'belly sticking out'. Seri babies in Mexico aren't given proper names until their first birthday, and their early nicknames - such as 'though he eats he isn't full' - are used until puberty.

POWER OF PROTECTION

Because a name is so closely associated with the self, giving the baby the right name can be crucial. According to North American folklore, the wrong name can cause a child to fall ill. Tibetan parents sometimes try to cure a sick child by asking an incarnate Lama to give a new name. In a sense, the name is seen as having magical qualities. Haitian babies are given two names in infancy; one must remain a secret between the parents until the baby is old enough to guard it for himself, lest it be used against the child in black magic. In parts of the world with high rates of infant mortality, anxious parents might give a child an ugly name - like 'Dung' in Hawaii, 'Dog Shit' in Tibet - in the hopes of discouraging evil spirits from taking the baby.

DISCOVERING BABY'S NAME

We talk about 'finding' a name; many people believe that since the child is a reincarnated ancestor, his or her true name must literally be discovered. How do you find the right name? Sometimes a list of ancestors' names is recited and the name being spoken when the baby begins to suck, for instance - or, amongst the Maori of New Zealand, when the child sneezes, since sneezing is seen as a communication from the spirits - decides the child's name. The Aborigine woman in Australia finds her baby's name during the last stage of the birth process, by reciting a list of possibilities until the moment the placenta is born. The Dyak of Borneo offer the baby a bundle of reeds with names inscribed on them and wait to see which one it touches.

WHAT'S IN A NAME?

Many people in different parts of the world name their babies after something that happened, or was seen at the time of birth: the Hawaiian name *Kapaulehuaonap-alilahilahiokaala* means 'the lehua flower blooming on the step ridges of Mount Kaala'. *Ellema*, a Gabbra name, means 'born when the camels were grazing in the high green grass'.

- The Bedouin name their children after parts of the body: *Al Sirra*, 'navel'; *Zib Sahman*, 'dog's penis'.

- Tibetans commonly name their children after their day of birth: *Nyma*, 'Sunday'; *Dawa*, 'Monday'; *Mingma*, 'Tuesday'.

- The Miwok Indians of California give their children nature names: *Kono*, 'a tree squirrel biting through the center of a pine nut'; *Iskemu*, 'water running gently when the creek dries'.

GODPARENTS

To Tennessee Williams, children were 'no-neck monsters', while William Wordsworth apotheosized the newborn infant as a 'Mighty Prophet! Seer Blest!' Most adults know the truth is somewhere in between. (Eloise Salholz)

Which people are named and linked to the child, and what will their role be during its life? Children who are baptized are linked with a godmother and godfather, though the link may be merely formal. The Siberian child will have his 'navel mother' and 'carrying mother' - the woman who cut the cord at birth, and the woman who carries the infant in its cradle, covered in a beautiful kerchief, from the birth hut to the big house where the child is presented to its father. The Thonga child of South Africa will always be close to its father's sister, who holds the child during the name-giving ceremony. The Dinka child of Sudan forms a lasting and intimate relationship with the midwife or *geem*, the receiver of God's gift to man. Throughout life, the child is expected to be respectful towards her, and she must be motherly towards the child. Likewise, the Gabbra child of Kenya can always find treats at the home of his *aku*, the midwife who delivered him or her, and will care for her with little gifts and ceremonial visits throughout life.

Nyinba elder with child. Humla, Nepal.

160

COMMUNITY CARE

Because hunter-gatherers are often on the move, families have to be kept small and, as in our own culture, there aren't so many relatives to help. Instead, the community is like a family. The Tchambuli child in New Guinea feeds at its mother's breast as she plaits reeds into sleeping-baskets. There are always a few women about to attend to its other needs, and it soon learns to address every woman in its mother's clan as *aiyai*, 'mother'. Amongst the Ongre Negrito of Little Andaman Island, women sometimes breastfeed each other's babies to help out.

BABY-KEEPERS

As the baby grows, and starts to be able to crawl away from its mother working in the field, someone in the family takes over caring for it during the busy hours of the day. Amongst the prosperous Ngoni of Malawi, young girls called *amoreri*, meaning 'to care for', are hired to look after babies while the women manage their households. Like nannies every-where, the *amoreri* form very strong attachments to their babies. 'Bu bu bu, the baby cries for its nurse and not for its mother', goes one of their songs.

In most agricultural societies the job of babysitting is given to girls of seven and older, usually sisters; in India babies looked after like this are called 'hip babies' because of the way the young girls carry them around while they play with their friends. Dinka babies in Sudan are cared for by young aunts or nieces, called 'baby-keepers'. In Taira, on the Pacific island of Okinawa, it's the old women who spend much of their time wandering around the village, grandchildren strapped to their backs while their mothers work in the fields nearby. If the child cries, it's given gruel or taken to its mother to be fed. Little boys and girls might bang tins for the baby or show it leaves for entertainment. Otherwise, nobody pays very much attention to it, but as it grows the child gradually joins the group of children playing, having learned from its perch all it needs to know about the rules of the game.

161

CARE TAKERS

In Manus society in the Pacific it's the father who cares for the child while the mother works in the mango grove. Some years ago the Swedish government, in co-operation with industry, came up with a plan to help mothers and father share in babycare. Both parents are offered shortened working hours with little loss in pay, so that both can at the same time carry on with their careers and enjoy their child.

In agricultural societies, mothers and fathers tend to be very busy from dawn till dusk, yet most of the burden of childcare falls mainly on a woman's shoulders. But because families are large and close-knit, there's always an older sibling, an aunt or a grandparent to help. 'Everyone helps', says Scherzoom, a Nyinba woman in Humla, Nepal. 'Mother-in-law, grandmas and grandpas, little brothers and sisters, husbands, but mostly the mother'.

When I turn my head
He smiles at me, my baby,
Hidden deep in my hood,
Oh, how heavy he is!
Ya, ya! Ya, ya! (Innuit lullaby, Greenland)

Carrying: Innuit mother and child in a parka built for two.

162

CARRYING

When we look back 8,000 years, we find evidence that our ancestors always carried their babies close to them. Further back along the evolutionary scale, small monkeys cling instinctively to their mothers' underbellies - the strong grip with which your baby holds on to your thumb is actually an undeveloped form of that same clinging reflex.

It's believed that baby-carrying devices may have been the earliest form of human tool. Some were made from animal skins - it was traditional in many cultures to give the new mother the skin of an animal sacrificed at the post-birth ceremony; today, the flowered red cloth carriers used by Chinese women are still shaped like animal skins.

INNOVATIVE DESIGN

Other people adapted their clothing to make it possible to carry the baby. An Inuit woman's fur parka is cut wider than a man's, and her baby traditionally rides naked inside it except for its caribou-skin nappy and its little cap, supported under its bottom by a sash tied round the mother. Tucked inside, it can hear its mother singing and is soothed as she hugs it close to her.

BACK OR FRONT ?

Some women like to carry their babies curled up or held tight with bands of cloth high against their backs, close to their centre of gravity; other women prefer a front position, especially for tiny babies - so that mother and child can feel closer to each other. The Indonesian baby sling, like the Mixtecan Indian rebozo, nestles the infant against the mother's belly and breast, comfortingly cradle-like.

MOBILE CHILD
DEVELOPMENT CENTRE

There are two classes of travel - first class, and with children. (Robert Benchley)

!Kung bushwomen carry their babies in slings at their sides as they search and dig for roots in the Kalahari Desert. The infant can curl up to sleep, rocked by its mother's movements. Waking, it can sit up and bounce, or play with its mother's hair and the beads round her neck, learning quickly how to reach and find her breast. The baby on the hip is at the same height as the fascinating world of older children, a constant source of entertainment.

Used on a daily basis, the sling serves as pram, playpen, rocking cradle, bouncing chair and infant seat rolled into one - a mobile child development centre.

THE BENEFITS
OF CARRYING

Studies in Uganda have shown that babies who are carried in upright positions are quicker to walk, and develop faster in other areas too; the upright position heightens a baby's

visual alertness while developing muscles in the back and neck. Carried around all day, babies become familiar with their worlds as they watch from their secure vantage point. Because they're held close and upright they stay calmer - studies show that they even cry less than babies that aren't carried regularly. Western mothers are discovering that the sling is not only a liberating means of transporting babies, but also a perfect solution to the dilemma of how to cook supper and at the same time soothe a baby during those fussy evening hours.

Baby and work are integrated in many mother's lives. Above: An Ovahimba woman takes her children shopping in changing Namibia. Left: A Senegalese mother and child. Right: A northern Thai mother and child. Far Right: New York Housewife, 1955.

GROWING UP

In most non-industrial cultures, children are allowed to be babies until another baby is conceived or born. The new baby will need its mother's milk and the shelter of her body, so by necessity the youngest child will have to give up these comforts and move a little further into the wider world. To wean the child, the mother might rub bitter herbs on her nipples.

The Ibo people of Nigeria call the newly weaned child 'the child who brought the child', and reward it for having separated itself from the mother, making the next baby possible. The long postnatal sex taboo amongst the Ibo and people in several other non-industrial societies means that each baby will have the shelter and nourishment of its mother's body for close to three years - the first phase of childhood during which, according to Western thinking on child development, babies form their main attachments in life and their basic trust in the world.

WEANING THE CHILD

- Czechoslovakian babies were once weaned with a touch of humour. The mother would bake a cake with a hole in the centre and put it on her breast, so that her nipple protruded through the hole. The child, laughing so much that it couldn't suck, would take the cake instead, and so the weaning process began.

- Many people encourage their babies to stop breastfeeding by stuffing their mouths with special delicacies: fish eyes amongst the Utku of Canada; Tchambuli children of New Guinea are given lotus stems, lily stems, and pieces of sugar cane.

- Hausa babies in Ethiopia are weaned in a single day - according to Muslim law, always on a Friday.

- Some people, such as Jamaicans, send the child off to Grandma's house for a couple of days so that it'll be apart from its mother and won't feel so frustrated about being denied her breast.

THE CHILD NOW KNOWS

Once the strong physical and emotional bonds have been made, children feel secure enough to start exploring the world beyond. Mixtecan Indians call this next stage in a child's life 'The child now knows'. According to Western theory, by this age children know who their mothers are, and that they still exist even when they're not in sight.

In cultures where parents expect children to grow up and repeat the lives their ancestors have lived for generations, everything can be learned by watching, listening, and playing. From its carrying sling, the !Kung child learns by the age of two or three all about the desert, its tracks, and the edible roots that can be found there, just as the Mbuti child in New Guinea learns about the forest, its vines and vegetables. Sitting by the fire at night, listening to adults telling stories, children absorb the lore of their culture, and learn about the hunt. Playing with little bows and arrows, they sharpen their skills.

Wodaabe children of Nigeria learn the ritual of tea-drinking at an early age.

Mother and child out fishing. St. Louis, Missouri.

CELEBRATING GROWTH

People all over the world trace and celebrate the growth and development of their children. We celebrate children's birthdays, both as a way of marking the passing of a year of life and all that has happened in it, and also to commemorate the event which brought this life into the world. But in many non-industrial societies, where parents have no calendars for marking the exact date of birth, a child's progress is measured by important physical events, and each of these events is cause for a feast, a ritual, a rite that symbolizes the child's passing from one state and being reborn into another. The most obvious of these are the puberty ceremonies - rites of passage from childhood into maturity - but in many cultures they're just the climax of a whole series of celebrations that start with the infant's passing from the world of spirits into the world of people.

In Samoa, for instance, it was traditional to hold feasts for 'the sitting of the child', 'the crawling of the child', 'the standing of the child', and a special feast with singing and all-night dancing for 'the walking of the child', for now the baby would pass from a totally dependent state and join the playing children. The Bantu people of South Africa celebrated the first time a child answered to its name. In the Yucatan, a ceremony called *Hets Mek* is held to mark the child's transition from being carried in arms to being carried straddling the hip.

The Chagga people of Uganda celebrate the baby's first tooth, which marks a new stage in life called, 'Now the child is complete'. The grandmother arrives, bearing special herbs which she rubs over the baby's gums with a blessing, to ensure a good set of teeth. Then baby is given its name and its first taste of solid food.

The baby's first haircut is marked with a ceremony and festivities in many cultures, for the cutting of the 'birth hair' as Tibetans call it, like the cutting of the cord at birth, symbolizes a child's severance from the mysterious other-world of the mother's body. On the Indonesian island of Roti, everyone feasts on a ritually slaughtered pig, and the baby's locks are hung in a palm tree - just as we might keep the first lock cut from our baby's head.

Everything about a new family takes time. But we all want to share our lives, don't we? Isn't that the most important thing?

FUTURE

There is an enormous amount children can teach us about ourselves. Who knows - maybe babies do come from falling stars, as the Indians in Guatemala believe. Maybe they do know more than we do. Maybe they are wiser, as the Hopi Indians believe.

When the Arapesh father welcomes his baby into the community he invokes the names of the village children and names pieces of yam after them, in the hope that his child will grow up to be hospitable and kind. For this baby will shape the world of the future.

What are your hopes for your child, for your child's future, for the shape of that future?

The Chinese speak of two kinds of cycles which mirror each other: the seasonal cycle, in which leaves brown, fall, and new leaves form just as new eggs replace fallen eggs in a woman's menstrual life; and the generational cycle of seed to fruit to seed. In becoming parents - not only sons or daughters, but fathers or mothers too - we become part of and responsible to that larger cycle, the continuous thread of time.

A baby is like the beginning of all things - wonder, hope, a dream of possibilities. In a world that is cutting down its trees to build highways, losing its earth to concrete, babies are almost the only remaining link with nature, with the natural world of living things from which we spring. (Eda J. Leshan)

AKNOWLEDGEMENTS

Endpapers: Sandra Lousada

Facing title page: Photo Sandra Lousada. Introduction: Photo Perilli Family collection. Photo Carol Beckwith. Contents Page: Photo Richard Browning *The Miles Quads*,1936.

Chapter One : I Came From the Sky

Frances Myers 6; Photo Thomas L. Kelly 9; Mawalan 1908-1967 and his eldest son 1927-1987. *Djang 'Kawu story*, Gift of Stuart Scougall 1959 Art Gallery of New South Wales 11; Tamara De Lempicka, Petit Palais Musee Geneve 13; Frances Myers 14; Photo Robert Doisneau, Rapho Agence de Pressee 15; Photo Jean-Louis Nou, *Gopis in Yamuna*, New Delhi Museum 16; Philadelphia Museum of Art, given by Mrs. William H. Horstmann 17; Photo Thomas L. Kelly 18; Smithsonian Institute, National Museum of Natural History Department of Anthropology 19 b.l.; Neil Barnden 19; Photo Jean-Louis Nou, *The First Glance*, Mrigavat Series Sultanate, Bharat Kala Bhavan, Varanasi 20; Photo Michael Freeman 21; Photo Laborie, Bergerac f.l. 22; Hermenegildo Bustos, Museo de la Alhondiga de Granaditas, Guonajuato 22; Photo John Sanday, Apa Photo Agency 23.

Chapter Two: Ten Moons Rising

Frances Myers, Neil Barnden 26,27; Frances Myers 29; Photo Sandra Lousada 31; The Royal Library, Windsor Castle 32; National Library of Medicine Bethesda, USA 34, 35; Photographie Giraudon 37; Frances Myers, Neil Barnden 38, 39; Photo Robina Rose, Co-Optic 40; Photo Sandra Lousada 42; ibid 44; Photo Sandra Lousada 46; Wellcome Institute Library 47; Photo Sandra Lousada 49; The British Library 50; Historical Monuments of England 52; Photo Gena Naccache from *Water Birth*, by Janet Balaskas & Yehudi Gordon, Active Birth Unit, Garden Hospital Hendon, London 52 t.m.; Photo Carol Beckwith & Angela Fisher 54; Photo Jean-Louis Nou *Love's Longing*, Patna Museum, Patna 55; Peter Beard 58; Photo Gena Naccache, *Adrianne in Early Labour*, Garden Hospital 59; Photo Sandra Lousada 60.

Chapter Three: Preparing the Nest

Neil Barnden 62, 63; Photo Sandra Lousada 65; Photo Thomas L. Kelly 66; Photo Carol Beckwith & Angela Fisher 67; Photo Art Whitman Black Star, Colorific 69; Photo Thomas L. Kelly 70; The Fine Arts Museum San Francisco, gift of Peter F. Young 72; Wellcome Institute Library 74, 75; Josephwitz Collection 76; University St. Andrews, Scotland 79; Photo Gena Naccache 80.

Chapter Four: The Baby Is At the Door

Frances Myers 82, 83; Frances Myers 85, The Hulton Picture Library 86; Photo Mary Motley Kalergis 87; Photo Marjorie Shostak, Anthro Photo 88; The National Library of Medicine, Bethesda, USA 89; Photo Gena Naccache *Adrianne in Labour*, 91; Photo John Ryle, Hutchinson Library 93; Photo Sandra Lousada 95; Photo Gena Naccache from *Water Birth*, by Janet Balaskas & Yehudi Gordon, Active Birth Unit, Garden Hospital Hendon, London 97; Photo W. Schneider-Schutz, Museum fur Volkerkunde SMPK, Berlin 99; Westermann, Friedrich von Zglinicki, Berlin 100-101; Photo Brian Lanker 102-103; Photo Jean-Gil Bonne 104; Photo Gena Naccache 106; Dumbarton Oaks Washington D.C. 108; Photo Gena Naccache (see p. 97)109; Metropolitan Museum of Art, The Michael C. Rockefeller Memorial Collection 110; Frances Myers 111; Photo Gena Naccache, *Joshua Bliss*, 112.

Chapter Five: Mamatoto

Frances Myers 114; Photo Gena Naccache (see p. 97) 117; Photo Thomas Bergman 119; Photo Mathias Oppersdorff 120; Photo Bruno Zehnder 121; Photo Thomas L. Kelly 123,124; The Mansell Collecton125; Richard Browning 126;Thomas L. Kelly 128; Statuette Artemis Ephesia, 200 AD, Indiana University Art Museum, Bloomington 130; The Mansell Collection 131; Photo Jean-Louis Nou, *When Spring's Mood is Rich*, Chandigarh Museum, Chandigarh 132; The Mansell Collection 133; Photo Carol Beckwith & Angela Fisher 134; Photo Frances Myers 135; Photo Carol Beckwith 136; Photo Sandra Lousada 137, 138; Photo Thomas L. Kelly 139; Photo Phillip Nelson, Art Unlimited, Amsterdam 140; Photo Smithsonian Institution, National Museum of Natural History, Department of Anthropology 141; Photo Mirella Ricciardi, from *Vanishing Africa* 142; The Mansell Collection 143; The Hulton Picture Co. 145; Frances Myers 146; Photo Andrea Singer, Hutchinson Library 147; Photo Carol Beckwith 148.

Chapter Six: A New Stranger Has Arrived

Neil Barnden 150-153; Photo Bryan and Cherry Alexander 154; Jean-Louis Nou 156; Photo Richard Browning 157-159; Photo Thomas L. Kelly 161; Photo Bryan and Cherry Alexander 162; Hans von Bartels 163; Photo Alain Nogues/Sygma 164; Photo Thomas Hegenbart, Stern, Hamburg 165 t.r.; Photo Michael Freeman 165 b.m.; Photo Elliott Erwitt, Magnum Photos, Inc 165 b.r.; Photo Carol Beckwith 166; Photo Thomas L. Kelly 168; Photo Kirsti Hilden 169; Michael Freeman 170.

BARBARA ARIA -
author

Barbara Aria is a British writer who has lived and worked in America since 1978. She is co-author with Caterine Milinaire of the highly successful book *Birth* (Harmony, 1987). She collaborated with child-therapist Dr Norma Doft on *When Your Child Needs Help: a Parents' Guide to Therapy for Children* (Harmony, 1991).

She combined her experience of childcare and design (she's written and edited illustrated books on architecture and design) to produce *Kid Style* (Fawcett/Columbine, 1987) and more recently, *Nursery Design* (Bantam, 1990), which addresses the subject of children's room design within various contexts including child development, the history of the family and domestic architecture, and the psychology of interior decoration.

Barbara Aria is an English Literature graduate from Sussex University, School of African and Asian Studies. She lives in New York and has a nine- year- old daughter.

CARROLL DUNHAM -
anthropological research

Born in New Jersey, and an anthropology graduate from Princeton, Carroll Dunham has spent the last six years in Nepal, running *Sojourn Nepal*, a school in cross-cultural education for American students. She and her husband, photographer Thomas Kelly, wrote *The Hidden Himalayas* (Abbeville Press, 1987).

Carroll Dunham's research on child care and the social role of women throughout the Himalayas and other cultures was essential to this book and the development of The Body Shop's mother-and-baby range of products, MAMATOTO.